From Sales Rep to CEO

Why Not You?

Joel Gaslin

FROM
SALES REP
TO
CEO

Why Not You?

JOEL GASLIN

From Sales Rep to CEO

1st Edition

Copyright © 2025 Joel Gaslin

ISBN: 979-8-9917616-3-5

TILT PUBLISHING

Tilt Publishing
700 Park Offices Drive, Suite 250
Research Triangle, NC 27709

Acknowledgements

This book is dedicated to Jean, my wife of 35 years, our four adult children and their spouses and significant others, and our grandson, Leo. I love you all, and am immensely grateful for each of you.

This book is also dedicated to my mentor, friend, and cousin, Paul Ehlen. You died too soon and you are missed. Thank you for all you did for my family and me.

Contents

Introduction

Why Not You?

Have you ever caught yourself staring out the window during a sales meeting, imagining a future where you're not just meeting quotas but leading the entire company? Maybe you've wondered what it would feel like to steer the ship instead of working the oars. You're not alone.

For years, I lived that question. As a sales rep, I dreamed of climbing the ladder—not just for the corner office or a bigger paycheck but to make a real difference. I wanted to influence strategy, create meaningful change, and help others reach their potential. That dream didn't happen overnight, and the road wasn't a straight line. It took decades of learning, unlearning, missteps, and breakthroughs. Ultimately, after beginning as a sales rep, I earned the title of CEO. And you can, too.

Here's the truth: The qualities that make an exceptional sales rep—resilience, customer focus, and relentless drive—are the very ones that can launch you into the C-suite. But the journey isn't just about working harder or selling more. It's about developing the mindset, skills, and vision of a leader while staying rooted in humility and service.

That's where this book comes in.

What You'll Get from This Book

From Sales Rep to CEO isn't your typical business book. It's not filled with abstract theories or advice you can't use. It's practical, actionable, and written for people like you—sales professionals who know they're capable of more but aren't sure how to get there.

Here's what you'll find inside:

- **Proven Strategies:** Learn the skills that CEOs use daily to lead, inspire, and grow their companies. From building a culture of transparency to crafting a vision for success, these strategies will elevate your career and your results.

- **Real-Life Stories:** You'll hear about my own journey, including what worked, what didn't, and the lessons I learned the hard way. You'll also meet others who made the leap from sales to leadership and learn from the insights they've shared.

- **Actionable Exercises:** At the end of each chapter, you'll find exercises designed to help you put the lessons into practice immediately. These aren't busywork—they're tools to help you grow as a professional and a leader.

- **A Blueprint for Growth:** Whether your goal is to become a CEO or simply be the best sales rep in your company, this book will give you a clear path to achieving it.

Why This Book Matters

There's a massive gap between the skills needed to sell a product and the skills required to lead a team or run a company. Closing that gap takes intention. It means understanding your numbers, aligning with other departments, and learning to see the big picture. It also means embracing humility—not as a weakness but as your greatest strength.

This book isn't just about titles or promotions. It's about transforming how you think about your work, your relationships, and your future. It's about becoming the kind of person others want to follow.

The book starts with the essential first step of forming a vision of becoming the CEO and highlights the importance of aligning that vision with a clear strategy and goals to achieve at each step of the way.

It then guides you through a journey that begins with understanding your own mindset and expands outward to encompass understanding your organization, all its key functions, and the environment in which it operates.

Finally, that journey returns to you, highlighting the key attributes of a leader that you must develop to transform yourself from sales rep to CEO.

Let's Begin

You're here because you're ready for something more. Maybe you've been in sales for years, wondering if there's a bigger role for you to play. Maybe you're already a high performer looking for your next challenge. Or maybe you've just started your career and want to aim for the top.

No matter where you're starting, this book will help you move forward. It's not going to sugarcoat the process or promise overnight success. But if you're willing to do the work, you'll discover that the path from sales rep to CEO is not only possible—it's within your reach.

So, let's get started. Because the question isn't *if* you can make the leap.

It's *why not you?*

PART ONE

Understanding Vision, Strategy, and Goals

The journey from sales rep to CEO is both transformative and challenging, requiring more than just sales acumen or technical skills. It demands a shift in mindset, away from pursuing short-term wins to focusing on a long-term vision for your own career. Alongside that vision, you'll need clear goals and a strategy to achieve them. As you transition into leadership, you'll need to embrace a broader perspective, learning to think not only about your immediate sales targets but also about where you want to take the company, how you'll get there, and the steps you need to take along the way.

In Part One, we will explore the critical components of that journey: developing a clear and compelling vision, crafting a strategic roadmap, setting actionable goals, and, most importantly, aligning all of them to drive both personal and organizational growth. Each chapter will provide the tools you need to start realizing your vision of transitioning from a successful sales rep to a star CEO.

1

From Goals to Greatness: The Power of Vision in Business

A clear vision isn't just for CEOs; it's a tool every sales rep needs to thrive and set themselves apart. Vision goes beyond daily tasks, beyond quotas, and turns an ordinary job into a purposeful journey. This chapter will guide you through understanding the role of vision in business and why learning to align with it now can prepare you for success later—even in the CEO's chair.

A Young Man Creates a Vision for His Career

In October 1991, two weeks past my 26th birthday, I wrote "The Twenty-Year Plan." I'd been in ophthalmology for half a year. The words I put down were rough, maybe naïve, but the drive was real. The plan was clear: By January 1, 2011, I'd be president and CEO of Storz Ophthalmics, Inc., and I'd have my seat on the American Cyanamid Board of Directors.

I laid out each step like a roadmap. I'd be a top performer, then earn an MBA in strategic management and climb the ladder rung by rung. I saw myself in new roles, moving from manager to director, then vice president, and finally CEO. Each milestone had a date. In my mind, it all seemed certain.

Today, I look back and grin at the young man who thought he'd reach the top in twenty years. It took more. But I eventually got there as president and CEO of a private equity-backed medical device company in ophthalmology. I led teams, drove growth, and carved out a path for the future of the business. The journey was longer and tougher, but the satisfaction went deeper than I'd ever imagined.

Why Vision Is the Foundation for Success

A vision in business is a map pointing to the future, a goal far enough to chase yet clear enough to see. A CEO's job is to create and share that vision, making it something the whole team can rally around. For a sales rep, connecting with this vision isn't just about doing their job—it's about understanding what makes their role essential to the bigger picture.

Without a vision, companies can feel like a boat without a rudder, pulled in every direction by market trends, customer demands, or internal politics. But with a clear vision, there's purpose, a sense of destination. Every effort, from top to bottom, ties into something larger, something shared. Imagine this: You're no longer just selling a product; you're part of a story that aims to improve lives and create value and impact.

Think of your role as a "CEO of your territory." When you understand the broader company vision, you can apply it to your region, customers, and goals. It helps you frame what you do as part of a larger goal, building more trust with customers who sense you're there for the long haul, not just the next sale. You're not only meeting targets but also forging partnerships based on a shared future.

At Sightpath Medical, for example, my first move as CEO was to launch Project BEGIN, a 100-day plan built around a company-wide vision. Each letter in BEGIN represented a goal—Build, Evolve, Grow, Imagine, New—and each piece linked to tangible, actionable steps. This vision didn't just live on paper; it pulsed through team meetings, strategy sessions, and even casual conversations. And as everyone saw their role within it, engagement grew, and results followed.

To harness this power as a sales rep, create a "vision" for your territory. Picture what success looks like—not just for you but for your customers and your company. When you share that future with your customers, it shifts your role. You're no longer just a seller but someone with a mission they can get behind. It's about showing them what they'll gain from your product and how they're part of something bigger.

This shift in mindset has its rewards. Customers trust and respect you more and are often more willing to work with you. It shows that you're not merely selling for the here and now but are invested in a future that benefits everyone. In time, that kind of thinking can set you apart, giving you a reputation as a sales rep who cares, thinks big, and delivers more.

Learning to Share a Vision to Sell More

In June 1991, I took my first job out of college, selling pharmaceuticals for Upsher-Smith Laboratories in Minneapolis. Upsher-Smith was small back then, primarily focused on selling a potassium chloride supplement to pharmacists and wholesalers over the telephone.

Soon after I started, we launched something new—a way for parents to bring down their children's fevers with an acetaminophen product that kids wouldn't fight against taking. We had flavored pellets to mix with food, a liquid children could drink, and a suppository for infants and older kids.

The products worked. Kids would take the flavored ones without a fuss, and the suppository took effect fast. Upsher-Smith's vision was simple: Make it easier for parents to help their kids feel better without the struggle. Anyone with kids knows what a relief that would be.

At first, sales were slow. "Another acetaminophen product?" buyers asked. Then I started talking to them about the vision behind it—the relief for parents, the ease for kids. Orders picked up, and I shared this with my small team. Soon, we were on a roll.

Early on, I learned that selling meant more than listing features; it was about sharing the "why." People want to buy if you give them a reason.

Key Takeaway: Vision Gives Everyone Direction

A well-defined vision gives a company and everyone in it a sense of direction. For you as a sales rep, understanding this vision is about more than just selling; it's about building something lasting. Embrace it, share it, and watch how it transforms your work and relationships.

Action Exercises

1. **Create Your Own "Territory Vision":** The objective of this exercise is to shift from meeting quotas to creating lasting value. Write down what success looks like for your territory in the coming year. Craft a statement that captures your long-term aspirations for growth and relationships. Then reflect on how having this vision changes the way you approach each customer.

2. **Communicate Your Vision to Customers:** To build stronger relationships based on shared goals, discuss your company's vision with a key customer and highlight how it aligns with their needs. Show them they're part of something bigger. After, note the response—did it shift their perspective?

3. **Lead Your Team or Peers with Vision:** To practice inspiring others, share your vision with your team and ask for their input. Discuss how aligning with this vision enhances performance. Observe how the conversation strengthens team dynamics.

2

The Secret of Real Success: How Strategy Can Turn a Sales Rep into a CEO

Every business has its day-to-day hustle, but the winners know that real success depends on something more profound: strategy. In this chapter, you'll learn what strategy means beyond buzzwords, why it's the difference-maker between a sales rep and a CEO, and how strategic thinking can change how you approach your territory, career, and future. Strategy isn't about quick wins but the more significant moves that build a lasting impact.

A Strategy to Build Demand and Eliminate a Competitor

In March 2013, I led a project at Sightpath Medical to bring a mobile femtosecond laser for cataract surgery to market. The LenSx laser had hit the market a year earlier after being acquired by Alcon, the biggest name in eye care.

At first, Alcon didn't want us mobilizing the laser. They figured people would shell out $375,000 without trying it first. But after a medical advisor urged them to reconsider, we got the green light. We adapted our patented method for mobilizing lasers to the LenSx and ran our first cases with Dr. Larry Patterson in Crossville, Tennessee.

What happened next caught us off guard. Instead of viewing the mobile LenSx as an easy way for surgeons to test the laser, Alcon's sales team saw us as competition. They figured we'd cut into their sales. This slowed adoption, and we had to pivot fast.

Two things needed to happen. First, we had to help Alcon convince surgeons they needed this laser. Second, we had to earn the trust of Alcon's field team—to get them to see us as partners, not rivals.

To meet the first goal, we launched a campaign called "How I Did It." The idea was simple: A panel of surgeons who used the LenSx shared stories about getting started. We used tried-and-true principles—social proof, authority, and likability—to spark interest in the technology.

For the second goal, we worked with Alcon's senior leadership to create a program called "Easy Start." It allowed their reps to bring in Sightpath's service for a trial period. Surgeons could try the laser and decide whether to buy one or keep using our service.

Both programs delivered. Adoption of the LenSx grew, and we shifted our relationship with Alcon from competition to partnership, paving the way for them to become channel sales partners instead of rivals.

Building a Strategy Mindset: Looking Beyond Today's Wins

Strategy is a blueprint in business that goes far beyond today's numbers. It's not about the latest sale or next quarter's results; it's about setting a direction that will matter months, even years, down the road. For a sales rep, seeing your role through the lens of strategy means thinking of your territory as a critical part of your company's journey, which can lead to leadership opportunities if played right.

Think of strategy as a way to answer three simple questions: Where are we now? Where do we want to go? And how do we get there? A strategic sales rep isn't just closing deals but actively shaping the company's path to its objectives. Each meeting, new relationship, and insight gathered from the field should connect to a bigger picture. It's about knowing the purpose behind each move.

Consider a surgeon deep in a procedure—each step has a specific goal, and each decision moves the patient toward recovery. Strategy in business is similar; every action has to work toward a larger purpose. When you're focused on strategy, it's not about hitting one sales goal after another but about making decisions that drive something lasting. To start thinking strategically, you might look at patterns in your sales data, spot trends that align with company priorities, and adjust your approach to create immediate and long-term gains. This strategic shift strengthens your reputation with clients and builds your standing in the organization.

This mindset is essential for anyone aiming to grow into the CEO role. CEOs are thinkers and doers who understand that action without direction is just busywork. A CEO doesn't just wonder, "How do we hit this quarter's target?" but, "How can we take steps now to be where we want to be in three years?" Shifting to this way of thinking builds resilience and foresight and ultimately positions you as someone who adds genuine value.

Look at the iconic companies that grew from a single idea to market leaders. Each had leaders who understood that building success wasn't about chasing every opportunity but about focusing on the right ones. Start thinking of your territory as a business within the business. When your strategy strengthens the organization's broader goals, you become more than a high performer; you become a driver of success and a natural candidate for leadership.

Strategy Must Be Built with Accurate Data and Insights

In late 2011, the CEO of Sightpath walked into my office—at the time, I was executive vice president of sales and marketing—and asked what I'd do with the sales team if I had unlimited resources. I've never liked that question. Resources are always limited. We tossed around some ideas and I didn't hear any more about it.

In early 2012, the CEO came back. Our private equity sponsors wanted help selecting a strategic planning firm to map out a five-year plan for Sightpath Medical. We interviewed a few firms, chose one, and got to work.

The firm's process was simple. They spent a day with me, another with Sightpath's head of operations, and just an hour with the CEO. A few weeks later, they came back with their plan.

I got a chance to review it over the weekend before they presented it to the board.

On Sunday night, I called the CEO and told him I saw a fatal flaw. He listened and agreed, but told me to let the firm move forward and work with the plan as it was.

The flaw was in what they called a "white space opportunity." They claimed Sightpath could double revenue in three years by expanding the sales team. They assumed that any surgical facility that did not perform cataract surgery was a potential client. They used our current procedural averages and pricing to create a number that excited everyone.

But they missed a key point: Ophthalmologists decide where cataract surgeries happen— not the facilities. You could ask a facility's administrator if they wanted to do cataract surgeries, and they'd say, "Sure. Bring me a surgeon who wants to operate here."

As the plan suggested, we built out our sales and marketing teams, doubling our commercial expenses. Three years later, we had to start dismantling them. Revenue hadn't kept up with our costs.

I learned a lot from that time. Whether working alone or with a team, I always scrub the data and assumptions before jumping to conclusions or making plans.

Key Takeaway: Strategic Mindsets Drive Lasting Success

Building a career isn't about tallying wins daily; it's about creating momentum toward a larger goal. Strategy is what separates those who merely perform from those who lead. As you've seen in these stories, a strategic mindset turns your work into a force for change within the company, pushing past today's results to build something enduring. Embrace strategy, and you're not just another sales rep—you're a leader in the making, carving out a path that can take you to the top.

Action Exercises

1. **Define Your Territory's Strategy:** Think of your sales territory as a mini business within the company. Identify three goals that go beyond short-term sales and directly support your organization's long-term growth.

2. **Map Out the Big Picture:** Consider one major objective your company has for the next three years and explore how your role can support it. This exercise can help you shape your approach with key accounts to align with broader company goals.

3. **Start with "Why?":** For your next sales initiative, ask yourself why it matters to the company's larger objectives. Write down your answer and see how it changes your approach, ensuring each step has a purpose beyond the immediate sale.

3

Bringing the Two Together: When Vision and Strategy Combine

Vision without strategy is a dream. Strategy without vision is chaos. This chapter shows how vision sets your direction and strategy charts the path, giving you the tools to thrive in business. Learn why sales reps need both vision and strategy to stay ahead, build momentum, and move toward the CEO role.

The Story of Eyeonics: A Vision That Changed an Industry

In the early 2000s, Eyeonics Inc., co-founded by J. Andy Corley and Dr. Stuart Cumming, set out to revolutionize cataract surgery with their groundbreaking product, the Crystalens. Dr. Cumming had been developing the technology for more than a decade, and it became the first FDA-approved accommodating intraocular lens (IOL) that allowed patients to focus at various distances. The Crystalens was designed to move within the eye, allowing patients to see clearly at near, intermediate, and far distances without glasses—unheard of with traditional cataract surgery lenses.

As Eyeonics built its vision around Crystalens, the company faced a significant challenge: Ensuring patients could access this premium technology while benefiting from Medicare coverage for cataract surgery. Traditionally, Medicare only covered standard IOLs, and patients could not pay the difference for a more advanced lens.

This restriction limited the adoption of innovative IOL technologies, including the Crystalens, because the costs were prohibitive.

To explore changing this, Andy Corley and the Eyeonics team worked closely with Christopher Cox, a former U.S. congressman and then SEC chair, to push for a patient-shared billing policy. The insight by Corley that Cox got approved was that the covered services in the reimbursement for cataract surgery did not include the correction of presbyopia (the need for reading glasses), which is what an accommodating IOL did.

This change, approved in 2004, allowed patients undergoing cataract surgery to choose premium IOLs like the Crystalens by paying more than the standard Medicare coverage. It also created a new revenue stream for ophthalmology practices that no one had imagined.

The approval of this policy was a game-changer for Eyeonics, the industry, and patients. It opened up new market potential by allowing patients to choose advanced lenses that improved their quality of life without forfeiting Medicare's financial support for cataract surgery.

This victory highlighted the importance of having a clear vision for product development, navigating complex healthcare regulations, and creating customer value. Eyeonics' vision extended beyond technical innovation; it involved understanding the broader industry landscape and finding a path to success through strategic collaboration and regulatory change.

The team's ability to work with Cox and other policymakers demonstrated that having a vision for the future of your product, combined with perseverance and creative problem-solving, can lead to groundbreaking achievements. The policy change ultimately helped Eyeonics grow, led to its acquisition by Bausch & Lomb in 2008, secured its place in ophthalmic history, and set a precedent for future medical device innovations.

The Compass and the Map: Finding Your Way in Business

Vision is what you see beyond the horizon—a place where you want to take your business. Strategy is how you get there. Imagine you're in a boat without a compass. You can paddle as hard as you like, but you'll end up either lost or circling back to where you started. Vision keeps you aimed in the right direction. Strategy guides each stroke, giving purpose to your efforts.

As a sales rep, it's easy to get caught up in the daily grind—calls, meetings, hitting numbers. But without vision, it's just noise. Vision gives meaning to your work. It's not about just dreaming big but seeing where you can make the most impact. Maybe it's expanding your territory, breaking into a new market, or becoming the go-to rep in your industry. Vision is personal, but it's never selfish. It drives you to build something bigger than yourself.

A good strategy takes your vision and turns it into reality. It's the difference between wishing for success and knowing how to get there. Strategy starts small, with steps you can control: identifying key accounts, building solid relationships, and planning your moves. Each action connects like links in a chain, pulling you closer to your goal. Strategy is disciplined. It means saying no to what doesn't serve your vision, no matter how tempting.

There's power in simplicity. Keep your vision clear, strip away what doesn't matter, and focus on what you need to get where you're going. A simple vision, backed by a solid strategy, is more potent than a complicated dream without direction.

Sales reps often focus on short-term wins; vision and strategy look beyond today. They ask: What do you want in the next six months? In a year? Five years? The reps who rise are those who see past the next sale. They understand that each conversation and relationship fit into a bigger plan. It's not just about selling a product but building a career.

Don't confuse tactics with strategy. Tactics are tools—pricing discounts, product demos, and email campaigns. They help, but they're not the plan. Strategy sets the course. It aligns with your vision, setting priorities that make sense over time. When you stick to a strategy, you build momentum. Each step is movement toward something that matters.

The strongest leaders start as strong visionaries. They're not afraid to imagine what's possible, and they also know how to make it happen. It's not about luck or talent. It's about putting the work in, day after day, with purpose. That's the road to the CEO's chair.

Xerox's Sales Vision

In the 1970s, facing growing competition from companies like IBM and Canon, Xerox transformed its sales vision and strategy. Instead of merely focusing on selling copiers, the company shifted its strategy to selling solutions that improved office productivity.

Xerox's sales reps were trained to communicate this new vision with their clients. They began positioning Xerox as both a copier company and a partner in making offices more efficient, productive, and profitable.

This shift in vision allowed Xerox to differentiate itself in a highly competitive market and ultimately regain its dominant position. Sales reps weren't just pitching machines anymore—they were pitching improved business outcomes.

Customers responded to this higher-level approach, and Xerox's new vision significantly contributed to the company's resurgence.

Key Takeaway: Steer Toward Success by Combining Vision and Strategy

Vision points you in the right direction; strategy keeps you moving forward. To thrive in business and grow toward the CEO role, find your vision, build your plan, and start rowing.

Action Exercises

1. **Define Your Vision:** Write down what success looks like for you in one year, three years, and five years. Make it specific.

2. **Build a Simple Strategy:** List three actions you can take next month that align with your vision.

3. **Evaluate and Adjust:** Set a reminder for three months from now to review your strategy. Adjust as needed to stay on course.

4

Steps Toward Your Vision: The Importance of Goals

You need more than a target when you're out there pushing through the noise and numbers. You need a map. This chapter teaches you how to build that map by weaving vision, goals, and strategy together. You'll learn how each piece works with the others and why every successful sales rep who becomes a CEO has mastered this balance.

Using Vision and Goals for Improved Collaboration and Alignment

At Sightpath Medical, we provided services to surgical ophthalmologists that reduced the headaches and costs of owning equipment, managing supplies, and maintaining expert surgical staffing for cataract and LASIK surgery. With over 85% of our employees in operations, their role was critical to supporting our service.

Early in my time at Sightpath, I noticed friction between the sales and operations teams. This tension impacted our ability to meet our company's vision and sales goals. It all came to a head during the annual budgeting process, which everyone loved to hate.

In my first year, we followed an established process driven by the CFO and supported by the sales team. The CEO would set a growth number for the company, and the sales reps would submit their projections for the upcoming year. The CFO would adjust average selling prices and cost inputs to match the annual growth goals. But this method created friction—especially with the operations team, who felt disconnected from the process and were often at odds with the sales projections, especially since their bonuses were tied to budgets they hadn't agreed on.

In the second year, we tried a new approach. We asked operations and sales leadership to collaborate and create an account-by-account budget. Both teams pushed back—it was a lot of extra work. But, by anchoring the conversation to the company's vision, we found common ground. When everyone understood the "why," much of the friction disappeared.

That year, we achieved better alignment between sales and operations, resulting in a more realistic budget and a collaborative approach. In the years to follow, this new process fostered deeper trust and helped us realize our company vision and annual goals.

Vision as Your Destination, Goals as Your Milestones, Strategy as the Path

The difference between vision, goals, and strategy is like that between a destination, milestones, and a path. It's simple, but if you miss one of these pieces, you might end up far off course. A vision tells you where you want to go, but it's hazy—it doesn't give you step-by-step directions. Goals are mile markers, measurable, and specific. And strategy? Strategy is how you plan to move from one goal to the next until you reach your vision.

Picture this: You're a sales rep with a vision to be the top performer in your region. That's good. It's where you want to end up. But without a route to get there, it's just a distant dream. You need goals. You might set a goal to increase your closed sales by 20% this quarter. Now you're getting somewhere. Your vision is in the distance, but your goals give you something concrete to reach for now.

So, where does strategy fit in? Strategy is your plan to hit those goals and keep moving toward that bigger vision. Maybe you'll focus on high-value clients first or sharpen your approach with decision-makers. Perhaps you'll spend more time on cold leads or leverage testimonials from happy clients. Whatever it is, strategy is your game plan, the moves you choose to get from one milestone to the next.

But why does this matter to a sales rep who dreams of being a CEO? Because setting goals and crafting strategy aren't just for the boardroom, they're for the battlefield. CEOs who started as sales reps knew how to balance their vision and goals and had the grit to put their strategy into action. They knew that vision alone wasn't enough to drive results unless they added clear goals and an intelligent strategy.

Here's the truth: You're measured by what you achieve, but your vision and strategy get you there. If you don't have a plan, your goals won't hold. If you don't have goals, your vision floats away. It's easy to set a sales target for the month, but it's more challenging—and more valuable—to set a vision for what you'll do in a year, three years, or even five. When you're aiming for that CEO chair, knowing how to combine all these elements is what sets you apart.

Remember, sales is about taking action with purpose. Every deal closed, every call made, each pitch delivered—these are steps on the path. And when you learn to make each action fit into a larger plan, you're not just a rep anymore. You're a leader with vision, goals, and strategy, moving purposefully toward your desired future.

How the "We Believe" Campaign Became the Touchstone for Sightpath Medical

In 2013 and 2014, times were tough at Sightpath Medical. We were undergoing a U.S. Department of Justice investigation, locked in a legal battle with a key distribution partner, and trying to launch a new service line that wasn't taking off as planned.

During those hard months, I read Simon Sinek's *Start with Why*. His message hit home: People don't buy what you do, they buy why you do it.

That idea stuck with me. I saw it as the seed for a campaign that could lift our spirits, align us on a vision, and remind us where we wanted to go.

I turned to Nicole Monacell, our director of marketing and unofficial director of culture. One morning, I walked into her office and wrote a list of core beliefs I thought we needed to succeed. We went back and forth, fine-tuning each point until we had six solid "We Believe" statements. Then we got to work.

We used those beliefs in videos and collateral and plastered them around the office. Soon enough, people started talking about them naturally—in meetings, with customers, and in their day-to-day interactions. With her knack for building culture, Nicole organized informal events and reminders to keep those beliefs alive and help us through dark days.

Once people understood the bigger "why" behind our work, they rallied around it and shared it with our customers, which helped build stronger relations with them and laid the foundations for our future growth.

Key Takeaway: The Power of Vision, Goals, and Strategy

You can't go anywhere without a clear vision of where you're heading. Your goals give your vision structure and your strategy makes it real. Vision, goals, and strategy—each one builds on the others, guiding you to the success you seek.

Action Exercises

1. **Describe Your Vision:** Write down your vision for your career five years from now. What do you want to accomplish?

2. **Define Your Goals:** Set three measurable goals for the next three months that move you toward that vision.

3. **Develop a Strategy for Each Goal:** What specific actions will you take to make progress each week?

PART TWO

Understanding Yourself

After establishing your vision to become a CEO, the essential next step in your transformation is to understand yourself and the mindset that will propel you forward. Moving from sales rep to CEO starts with a shift in how you approach challenges, opportunities, and personal growth. Drawing on the work of Carol Dweck, the following chapters explore the power of a growth mindset—where progress is valued over perfection and every setback is seen as a chance to learn.

Just as important is developing an ethos of service, recognizing that true leadership is not about being in charge, but about helping others succeed. That mindset—focused on results, driven by opportunities, and grounded in service—will become your foundation as you evolve into a leader who inspires both trust and achievement.

Understanding yourself in this way is not just a personal transformation but a necessary step in your journey to becoming the kind of CEO who shapes the future of their organization.

5

Every Obstacle Is a Learning Opportunity: Why a Growth Mindset Is Essential

In the world of sales and leadership, success isn't just about numbers. It's about how you view challenges, setbacks, and your own abilities. Do you see obstacles as proof of limits—or as opportunities to learn? This chapter will help you understand the power of a growth mindset and how embracing it can propel you toward personal and professional transformation.

Not Yet, But Close

In her bestselling book *Mindset*, Carol Dweck tells the story of a Chicago high school where failure didn't exist—at least not in the usual way. Students who didn't pass a course weren't given an "F."

Instead, they received the grade of "Not Yet."

It wasn't just semantics. It was a mindset shift. "Not Yet" told students they hadn't succeeded yet—but they could. It turned failure into progress and pushed them forward instead of holding them back.

That idea stuck with me. In sales—and in life—it's easy to label a setback as a failure. A long sales cycle feels endless. A deal that doesn't close feels like a loss. You hear "no" enough times, and you start to believe it.

But what if you didn't see it as failure? What if you saw it as "Not Yet"?

Years ago, as vice president of sales and marketing for a medical device company, I faced this challenge with my team. Our reps were grinding through long sales cycles. Weeks turned into months and deals still weren't closing. Frustration mounted.

I hadn't read Dweck's book at the time, but the principle was the same. To keep the team moving forward, I introduced "Little Wins."

Instead of focusing on the finish line, we celebrated the steps along the way. Scheduling a demo was a win. Getting a second meeting was another. Each stage became its own victory.

It worked. Reps stayed motivated. Momentum built. Deals started to close.

"Not Yet" and "Little Wins" aren't just ideas. They're lifelines. When success feels far away, they remind you to keep going. The end isn't here—yet—but you're getting closer.

The Two Mindsets That Shape Your Career: Growth and Fixed Thinking

Some people see their abilities as unchangeable, locked in from birth. They might say, "I'm just not good at that" or "I was never cut out for leadership." That's the fixed mindset talking. It builds walls around potential, stifling growth before it begins.

Others approach life differently. They see every challenge as a stepping stone. Failures become lessons, setbacks become fuel. This is the growth mindset—a belief that skills can be developed, knowledge expanded, and success earned through effort.

Why does this matter for sales reps? Because growth mindset thinking is the difference between stagnating at quota and climbing to the CEO's office.

What Happens When You Embrace a Growth Mindset

A growth mindset doesn't just make you feel good; it changes how you work. Here's why it matters:

- **Resilience Against Rejection:** In sales, rejection is as common as coffee breaks. A fixed mindset internalizes rejection as failure: "I'm just no good at this." But a growth mindset reframes rejection as "Not Yet." Each "no" is a chance to refine your pitch, understand the customer better, and improve.

- **Continuous Improvement:** When you believe you can get better, you seek out ways to do it. That might mean asking for feedback, reading about new techniques, or shadowing a top-performing colleague. It's this relentless hunger for growth that sets leaders apart.

- **Innovation in the Face of Change:** Sales and business are constantly evolving. A growth mindset helps you adapt, whether it's learning a new customer relationship management (CRM) system or understanding a disruptive competitor. Instead of resisting change, you lean into it, finding ways to turn uncertainty into opportunity.

Practical Steps for Sales Reps

- **Turn "Failures" Into Feedback:** Start treating every lost deal or missed quota as a learning experience. What went wrong? What could you do differently next time?

- **Seek Challenges, Not Comfort:** Stretch yourself with tough customers, new markets, or unfamiliar products. Growth doesn't happen in your comfort zone.

- **Celebrate Progress:** Don't just measure success by big wins. Celebrate the small milestones—the steps that move you closer to mastery. The best sales reps and leaders don't believe they've arrived. They believe they're always arriving, always growing.

The Growth Test

My mentor in ophthalmology and selling (and in many personal ways) was Paul Ehlen, who hired me to run a business he owned while he focused on running another.

Precision Lens was a small, regional ophthalmic distribution company. Four independent reps sold two products, bringing in about $2.5 million a year. Paul owned the company with a partner but had recently bought him out. He liked the steady income but wasn't especially focused on the company; his attention was elsewhere.

Not long after I started as vice president and general manager, Paul and I spent a weekend in strategic planning with a consultant. Early in the meeting, Paul said something that caught me off guard. He told us he was satisfied with the company's size. All he cared about was that it kept producing enough income to cover the loan payments from buying out his partner.

I was surprised. This wasn't the Paul I knew. He wasn't the kind of man to settle. Growth had always been his way.

I spoke up. "If we're not growing, we're falling behind. Costs go up. Margins shrink. Staying still is moving backward."

The consultant, an accountant who knew Paul well, nodded in agreement. Paul listened, silent for a moment.

Looking back, I think Paul was testing me. He wanted to see if I was satisfied with standing still—or if I had the drive to push forward. We didn't use words like "fixed mindset" or "growth mindset" back then, but that's what it was about.

The weekend became a turning point. By the time it ended, we had an aggressive strategic plan in place. Over the next 11 years, that plan transformed the company.

Key Takeaway: Growth Over Perfection

Mindset isn't just a buzzword, it's the foundation of success. The ability to grow through challenges, learn from mistakes, and stay curious will not only elevate your sales career but also prepare you for leadership. The fixed mindset fears failure, but the growth mindset turns it into fuel.

Action Exercises

1. **Reframe a Setback:** Write down a recent failure or rejection. Next to it, write one thing you learned and one step you can take to improve.

2. **Challenge Yourself:** Set a goal to tackle a project or customer that feels intimidating. Track your progress and reflect on what you learned.

3. **Feedback Loop:** Ask a colleague or mentor for feedback on one area of your performance. Use it to create a specific action plan for growth.

6

Developing Yourself by Serving Others: The Power of a Service Mindset

Your journey to the CEO's office begins with a choice. Will you focus solely on hitting your numbers, or will you prioritize the people who make those numbers possible? The sales reps who become great leaders understand this simple truth: Serving others leads to greater success.

In this chapter, you'll learn how adopting a service mindset transforms not only your career but also the lives of those around you. It's the key to building trust, fostering loyalty, and creating value for customers, colleagues, and yourself.

The Quiet Power of Service

Let me tell you a story that taught me the true meaning of service.

I was interviewing Paul, a surgical technician with a military background, for a promotion. Paul was everything you'd expect from someone with his training—sharp, disciplined, and respectful, though his presence carried an edge that could make anyone sit up straighter. He didn't waste words, and every answer felt deliberate, like he was taking apart and reassembling a machine in his mind before speaking.

The interview was nearly over when I leaned back in my chair and decided to throw out one last question. It wasn't on the list, but something about Paul made me curious.

"Paul," I said, "which is more important to you: being right or being of service?"

He didn't answer right away. Instead, he held my gaze, his expression unreadable. I could see the gears turning as if he were weighing the question, not just for me, but for himself.

After a moment, he nodded slightly, as though he'd reached a conclusion. "Well, Sir," he said, his voice steady, "I can't always be right. But I can always be of service."

He delivered the words simply, without flair. Yet they hit with the weight of something undeniable. It wasn't just an answer, it was a principle he lived by. In that moment, I realized the question had been for me as much as for him.

I thought about how often people get caught up in being right—in proving themselves, winning arguments, or showing they're smarter. But Paul's answer cut through all of that. Being right is temporary; being of service is lasting. It's the kind of choice that changes not just how you work but how you live.

That interview ended with a handshake, but Paul's words stayed with me long after he walked out the door. What struck me wasn't just his clarity but the quiet conviction behind it. He didn't need to explain or defend his answer. It simply was.

I then understood something I hadn't before: To be of service is to choose humility. It's about putting others first, even when no one's watching. It's about showing up, not for the credit but for the contribution.

Paul didn't just teach me a lesson in service. He reminded me what leadership, at its core, is really about.

The Power of Service: Why It Matters

The best sales reps aren't just salespeople—they're trusted partners. They don't pitch products; they solve problems. They don't look for quick wins; they build relationships that last. This is the essence of a service mindset: Putting others first to create value that extends beyond a single transaction.

Think of your customers. Each one has goals, challenges, and pressures. They're not looking for a vendor; they're looking for someone who can help them succeed. When you step into that role, you go from being a salesperson to being an indispensable partner.

The same goes for your colleagues. Whether it's operations, marketing, or finance, every department in your company is a potential ally. But allies aren't born—they're made. When you approach internal relationships with the same service-first mentality, you build trust and create a culture of collaboration. That culture doesn't just make your job easier—it makes the entire organization stronger.

As you grow in your career, this mindset will become even more critical. CEOs don't just serve customers; they serve employees, shareholders, and communities. By practicing this early, you'll set yourself apart from peers who are solely focused on personal success.

Adopting a service mindset requires three things: curiosity, empathy, and action.

- **Curiosity:** Learn everything you can about your customers and colleagues. What keeps them up at night? What excites them? When you understand their world, you can find new ways to create value.

- **Empathy:** Step into their shoes. See challenges from their perspective. Empathy isn't just a nice-to-have—it's the foundation of trust and loyalty.

- **Action:** Service is a verb. It's not enough to understand needs; you must act on them. Anticipate problems. Offer solutions. Follow through on promises.

The reward for this effort isn't just professional success; it's personal fulfillment. When you know you've made someone's life easier, work becomes more than a job—it becomes a purpose.

The Simple Game: A Lesson from Paul Ehlen on Keeping Promises

During my first week as a sales rep in ophthalmology, I had an experience that shaped my career.

Paul Ehlen, my mentor, gave me a gift I didn't fully understand at the time: a full week of his time. He drove me around, introducing me to ophthalmologists he'd known for years, opening doors I could never have opened on my own.

It wasn't just the introductions that mattered. Paul's endorsement credentialed me as someone worth knowing in the industry. He didn't just bring me into the room; he made it clear I belonged there. His belief in me added weight to every handshake, every conversation, and every promise I made.

But the most valuable part of that week wasn't the handshakes. It was the time in the car with Paul. If you ever knew Paul Ehlen, you'd know he wasn't one to hold back on ideas or opinions. His passion for business and selling filled the car like the hum of the tires on the road.

He talked, I listened, and I learned more than I could have from any sales training manual.

There was one lesson that stuck with me above all others. We were driving down a lonely stretch of Highway 2 between Duluth and Grand Rapids, Minnesota. The trees crowded the road, their shadows stretching long in the afternoon light. Paul glanced at me, his hands resting casually on the wheel, and said, "You know something, Joel? Sales is a simple game. It's simple because all you have to do to succeed is do what you said you'd do, when you said you'd do it. You win because so few sales reps actually do that."

The silence hung in the air after he said it, the kind of silence that lets a statement sink deep. At the time, it felt almost too simple. Wasn't there more to sales than that? But over the years, I've come to realize the depth of what Paul meant. Doing what you say you'll do is more than just a way to close deals; it's a way to be of service to others.

Keeping promises shows your customers that you value their time, their trust, and their goals. It's not about just meeting expectations—it's about exceeding them in a way that makes people feel heard and understood. When you deliver on your word, you're not just fulfilling an obligation; you're building a relationship. And relationships, more than anything else, are what create lasting value.

This idea has guided me through countless situations, both good and bad. When I've honored my word, I've seen how it earns loyalty and opens doors to opportunities I could never have forced. And when I've fallen short, I've learned the hard way how quickly trust can erode.

It's a simple belief, yes, but it demands discipline, self awareness, and a mindset of service.

Sales isn't about manipulating people or pushing products; it's about helping others solve problems and achieve their goals. Paul's advice—to do what you said you'd do, when you said you'd do it—anchors you in that mindset. It reminds you that every interaction is a chance to deliver value, not just in the product or service you're offering but in the way you treat people.

That one piece of advice has served me more than any strategy or script. It's simple, yes. But simple doesn't mean easy. Doing what you said you'd do, when you said you'd do it, is a promise not just to your customers but to yourself. It's a commitment to be reliable, consistent, and, above all, of service.

Paul's words stayed with me long after that week ended. They've been a guide through the challenges of sales, business, and life. And every time I find myself veering off course, I think of that empty highway, the clarity of his wisdom, and the profound truth of how delivering on promises is the best way to deliver value.

Key Takeaway: Service Is the Foundation of Success and Leadership

A service mindset isn't just a strategy—it's a way of life. When you focus on helping others succeed, you unlock opportunities that would otherwise remain hidden. Serve well, and you'll not only elevate others—you'll elevate yourself.

Action Exercises

1. **Improve Your Customer Service:** Write down three ways you can better serve your best customers this month. Implement one of these ideas immediately.

2. **Serve Your Colleagues Better:** Identify one internal colleague who supports your work. Ask them how you can make their job easier.

3. **Become an Active Listener:** Spend a week practicing active listening in every conversation. Make sure you truly understand the other person's needs before responding.

7

From Me to We: Adopting a Results-Oriented, Opportunity-Driven Mindset

As a sales rep, hitting your numbers and contributing to your company's revenue is fundamental to your job. However, the leadership journey, and ultimately the CEO role, requires a shift in how you view results and your contributions. It's about thinking beyond your sales targets and seeing the broader impact your actions can have on the entire organization. In this chapter, we'll explore how adopting a results-oriented, opportunity-driven mindset can set you on the path to becoming a CEO.

The Sales Rep Who Thought Like a CEO

In my early days with Storz Ophthalmics, I got promoted and moved from the familiar streets of Minneapolis to the vast stretches of Upstate New York. My new territory spread from Erie, Pennsylvania, to Syracuse and Elmira. Long drives and empty files. The former rep hadn't left much for me to work with, just as I'd found before. Storz had a habit of handing over blank slates, but Sam Alioto, our VP of sales and marketing, had a plan to fix it.

It was the early nineties, before CRM systems or anything close to the tools we know now. Sam put a woman named Myrna in sales operations on a project to centralize data on surgeons and their facilities. The plan had potential, but it was slow work. Most reps saw it as a hassle, a chore they didn't need.

Once I'd settled in, Myrna called me. She asked if I'd received the project materials. I hadn't—the previous rep had tossed them—so she explained the vision behind it all: To streamline our work and to give us a better shot at sales. She talked about Sam's drive to make the system work and how hard it was getting the reps and managers to take the project seriously. I told her about a system I'd developed on my own in my last territory, something I called the Zone System. Myrna liked it. I said it could be just what the project needed and asked her to run the idea by Sam, and if he agreed, I'd act as the field advisor. Sam did, and just like that, I was part of something bigger.

We worked through it, step by step, creating a system that finally made sense to the sales reps and marketing. It was a look into the future of sales management, a hint of what was to come. I saw that my choice to lean in, help someone else hit their targets, and build for long-term efficiency was a good one.

When it was done, Sam was pleased. I had done well, though it would be about a year before I'd see how much it would matter for my career at Storz.

Results and Contributions: The Mindset of Future Leaders

In any sales role, results matter. But to truly grow into a leadership position, you must think beyond short-term wins and focus on contributions that impact the entire organization. Results aren't just about sales numbers—they're about how your efforts help your company grow sustainably. This is where Peter Drucker's philosophy, "The purpose of business is to create a customer," comes into play. As a sales rep, you're at the frontline of customer creation. However, future CEOs recognize that it's not just about creating a customer; it's about fostering a customer relationship that contributes to long-term business success.

Start thinking like a CEO by asking yourself these questions: Are you building relationships that support your company's broader vision? Are you collaborating across departments to ensure that your contributions help the company as a whole, not just your sales territory? When you begin operating with this mindset, you elevate your role from simply closing deals to contributing to the company's overall health. This is how leaders are made.

Business Turbulence Leads to Collaboration and Victory

The go-to-market model for Sightpath Medical in the Upper Midwest relied on an independent sales group owned by one of our founders. They sold our services and handled accounts. But late in 2014, they walked out and set up a rival company after a contract dispute.

They knew our pricing, our delivery schedules, and even our routes. They controlled the supply of many of the products we used. They had it all, except one thing—the surgical techs who kept close ties with our customers. But we had a problem. The sales group who controlled thirty percent of revenue had just walked out the door.

We moved fast. We hired two new reps, trained them, and sent them out alongside our operations team to secure every account we could. The two of them proved something: They showed the operations team and the rest of our sales force how valuable our techs were in keeping us afloat.

As those two reps gained ground, we didn't lose the customers we thought we would. The collaboration at each account and the teamwork between operations and sales did more than just fend off a threat; it tightened the bond between the two teams, setting us up for years of success.

Key Takeaway: Shift Focus from Yourself to Your Company

By shifting your focus from individual results to company-wide contributions, you set yourself on the path to leadership. A sales rep who builds relationships, seeks opportunities beyond the immediate sale, and understands their impact on the broader business is well on their way to thinking like a CEO. Embrace this mindset, and you'll hit your sales targets and contribute to long-term success for yourself and your company.

Action Exercises

1. **Evaluate Your Contributions:** Reflect on a recent sale and consider how it contributed to the broader success of your company. Write down three ways you could have improved the outcome by collaborating with other departments.

2. **Start Building Cross-Department Relationships:** Schedule a meeting with a colleague from marketing or operations. Discuss how their work impacts your role and brainstorm one way you could collaborate more effectively.

3. **Think Long-Term:** Identify a client with whom you can build a stronger, long-term relationship. Outline three steps you can take over the next six months to deepen that relationship and create more value for your company and the client.

PART THREE

Understanding Your Organization

As you continue your journey from sales rep to CEO, it's essential to broaden your perspective by understanding the inner workings of the entire organization, especially its culture and systems. This section will explore the importance of organizational culture in shaping the success of the company, and how embracing a cohesive, values-driven culture can drive performance at every level. Additionally, we'll dive into the Zone Selling System, a powerful framework that can guide your sales strategies while fostering alignment across the organization.

Balancing short-term objectives with long-term success is another key challenge that you'll need to master, ensuring that day-to-day wins contribute to the broader vision. Finally, building effective systems and processes will be critical as you scale the business and transition from managing a team to leading an organization.

By focusing on these elements, you'll be laying the foundation for sustainable success and positioning yourself to lead with both purpose and precision.

8

More than Just a Feeling: Why Culture Means Everything

We've all been there, walking into a company for the first time and getting "that feeling." Maybe it's the upbeat energy of the people buzzing around the office, or it could be the thick tension you feel as employees quietly shuffle from meeting to meeting with furrowed brows. That feeling, positive or negative, is your first taste of corporate culture.

Corporate culture may be intangible, but it's crucial. It permeates everything an organization does—the good, the bad, and the ugly— and understanding how you can create and change a culture is an essential step on the road from sales rep to CEO.

The Culture That Nearly Crashed My Career

During my final semester of college, I worked with a local lawn-care services company to test the waters of sales. Little did I know, I was entering a "sink or swim" environment.

On day one, they handed me a phone and a list of people to call. There was no training, collaboration, or shared vision. It was every person for themselves, like *Lord of the Flies* in real life.

I watched a talented guy named Brian burn out within three months. Despite his natural sales skills, the toxic culture drained him. This experience nearly drove me away from a career in sales altogether.

The Culture That Saved Me

Contrast what you read above with my experience at Upsher-Smith Laboratories, the small pharmaceutical company I joined later. From day one, our sales team was united in camaraderie and collaboration.

My manager invested time in training me and understanding my strengths and weaknesses. We shared wins, losses, and strategies in regular team huddles. When someone hit their target, we all celebrated. When someone struggled, we pitched in to help.

The difference was night and day—not because I suddenly became a better salesperson, but because I was in a culture that empowered rather than drained me.

What Is Corporate Culture?

Corporate culture is the unseen framework that dictates how a company operates daily. It influences decisions, how people treat one another, and how much joy or dread employees feel about going to work each morning.

Think of it like a recipe. The ingredients—the company's values, traditions, leadership style, and employee behaviors—blend to create a unique flavor. And just like a good meal, everything works when the culture is healthy. When it's off? Everyone can tell, and it generally shows in results.

Why Should a Sales Rep Care About Culture?

Many sales reps think, "I'm here to sell—what does culture have to do with me?" The short answer: everything.

The corporate culture you experience at your company can make or break your success. It shapes how you're supported, the tools you're given, and the kind of teamwork you experience. All these combined create an operating environment for running your territory.

You are more likely to succeed when you feel supported, included, and inspired by your daily interactions with your work colleagues and customers. By modeling that behavior, you become a leader by reflecting on what you experience in your company culture and demonstrating it to those around you.

But what happens if your company has a poor culture? What do you do then?

Stay positive, seek to understand what is causing the current culture, and begin working toward changing the environment. A situation like this can be an unexpected opportunity to establish yourself as a force for positive change—like every great leader!

The Foundation of Corporate Culture: Leadership

Corporate culture begins at the top. Leadership sets the tone, whether you're at a startup or a Fortune 500 company. The CEO, executives, and managers are responsible for crafting the values and behaviors that will filter down throughout the organization.

It's not enough for leaders to say, "Our culture is about teamwork and integrity." Those values have to be lived. If your manager says they value collaboration but then pits you against your colleagues in a cutthroat competition, that signals dissonance between stated culture and lived culture.

For sales reps, the role of leadership in culture is crucial. A supportive leadership team will give you the tools and training to succeed, they'll listen to your feedback, and they'll create an environment where you feel valued. Without a healthy corporate culture, you're left to fend for yourself in a chaotic, disjointed system—and trust me, that's not where you want to be.

How You Can Shape Culture as a Sales Rep

While leadership drives the overall direction, each person within the company contributes to the culture in some way. Your attitude, interactions with colleagues, and interactions with your manager all shape your day-to-day experience working in that company. Here's how you can actively influence and thrive within your corporate culture:

- **Lead by Example:** Even if you're not in a leadership position, you can set the tone by how you carry yourself. Be the person who collaborates, helps others, and embodies the values you want to see. Culture is contagious, and others will follow when you lead with positivity.

- **Communicate Openly:** If you see areas where the culture could improve, speak up. Have candid conversations with your manager about how you're feeling and what you think could enhance the team's dynamic.

- **Find Your Tribe:** In every company, some people align with your values and mindset. Seek them out and form a support network.

- **Own Your Growth:** No matter the culture, you always control your personal and professional development. Seek mentorship, invest in your skills, and focus on your goals. You can succeed even in challenging environments with a growth mindset.

Zone Selling: Building a Culture to Own Your Territory

When I first entered medical device sales in 1991 with Storz Ophthalmics, my territory spanned from Minnesota to South Dakota, North Dakota, Wisconsin, and the Upper Peninsula of Michigan. It was massive, stretching east to west from Rapid City, South Dakota, to Milwaukee, Wisconsin. That's a lot of miles, with few people in between.

With a new wife, a baby at home, and a hunger for success, I had to strategically cover this vast area. I quickly realized that if I didn't manage this territory, it would eventually manage me.

My first manager, Brian Reinkensmeyer, was critical in helping me build a system to tackle the region. Brian often asked, "When will you do that, Joel?" I'd give myself some leeway in my response, but he'd cut through, saying, "Do it today." At first, that frankness surprised me. Later, I understood that Brian's insistence on immediate action was a lesson in getting things done.

The Zone Selling System

The Zone Selling System brought order to the chaos of managing a large territory. It helped me take control rather than letting the territory dictate my schedule. The system revolves around simplicity, regular contact strategies to foster strong connections, and a commitment to follow-through that builds trust and loyalty.

It's not just about pre-call and post-call planning or staying organized. Zone Selling is a discipline: Doing what you say you'll do when you say you'll do it. It's a way to stay ahead of what's happening, seize opportunities, and succeed as a sales rep.

This system is as strong as the thinking behind it and your dedication to executing it. When set up right, it aligns with your sales goals, personal goals, and business needs, serving as a guide to visualize your path forward. In practice, it's about analyzing where you are today and how to get to where you want to be.

What is the Zone Selling System?

The Zone Selling System divides your territory into four zones. Start with these four to keep it simple, aligning with the four weeks in a month. Begin by marking these zones on a calendar for the next four months.

Each week, one zone becomes your focus for travel, prospecting, and account management.

Some might question this, thinking they can't plan that far out with calls, emergencies, and unexpected opportunities constantly popping up. Here's the truth: You'll never know exactly what's coming. However, discipline in protecting your work plan and following it is crucial.

Ask yourself, "Was that 'emergency' call urgent, or could more discovery work have helped? Could operational support have provided the solution instead of rushing out immediately?" With Zone Selling, you stay true to your plan without getting sidetracked.

Zone Selling in Action

At one point in my career, I used this system as a "player-coach." My role was complex, but I needed a dependable system to keep me moving forward, grow my territory's revenue, and achieve my goals.

Zone Selling is a flexible, proven method that works across territories, large or small. During the eleven years I used this approach, I grew revenue by over 500%. The system works; I'm living proof of it.

Initially, my Zone Selling System had four zones. But as my business grew, I added a fifth to serve my clients better and meet my objectives. This extra zone, based around the Twin Cities' dense population, let me plan with more fluidity. The addition also served our contract with a large integrated health delivery network in Minnesota, creating the need for a "flex week" to adapt to the network's demands.

I adjusted to a five-week rotation, synchronizing my calendar and structuring my travel, prospecting, and follow-up accordingly.

Key Takeaway: Shape Culture to Fuel Your Success

Corporate culture might seem intangible, but its effects are fundamental and far-reaching. As a sales rep, your culture can either accelerate your success or hold you back. While you might not have the power to change the culture overnight, you can influence it through your actions, mindset, and how you show up to do your work. The most successful sales reps excel because they're good at closing deals and understand how to navigate and shape the culture around them.

Action Exercises

1. **Evaluate Your Current Company Culture:** Take 30 minutes to write down what your company's culture feels like to you. Consider how people interact, how decisions are made, and what behaviors are rewarded or discouraged. Identify one thing you like and one area where you think the culture could improve. Share your insights with a trusted colleague or manager to discuss how these cultural aspects affect the team's performance.

2. **Lead by Example:** Pick one value you want to embody within your team: collaboration, positivity, or transparency. Over the next week, practice this value in your daily interactions. For example, offer to help a colleague with a challenge or openly share a sales strategy that worked for you. At the end of the week, reflect on how your behavior influenced the team. Did others start to mirror the value? Write down your observations and continue leading by example.

3. **Build a Culture of Feedback:** Identify an area for improvement related to company culture (e.g., communication, collaboration, etc.). Ask two colleagues for specific feedback on this area. Be open to both positive and constructive insights. Based on their input, set one actionable goal to improve your contribution to the team's culture. For example, if communication was highlighted,

commit to sharing regular updates with your team or asking more questions during meetings. Track your progress over the next month, noting any changes in your interactions with others and how these affect team dynamics.

9

Short-Term Action, Long-Term Traction: The Importance of Balance in Sales

Sales reps often face constant pressure to perform and meet immediate targets, but the ones who balance short-term wins with long-term vision are the ones who find lasting success. In this chapter, you'll learn how to align short-term actions with a long-term sales strategy, why both approaches are essential, and how to implement this balance to become a better rep and, ultimately, a CEO.

The "Ride-Along" That Changed My Career

If you've been in sales long enough, you know the drill. The call or email from corporate says, "So-and-so wants to ride along with you in three weeks." You think, "There goes a week of getting things done."

But in October of 1993, that call turned into a turning point for me.

I'd been working Upstate New York for fourteen months. I'd won Rookie of the Year the year before and was having a good but not great year. The call came from Robin, the assistant of Storz' vice president of sales and marketing, Sam Alioto, about a ride-along in two weeks.

I called my manager and a few sales reps, asking how to handle working with Sam. They said to keep it simple: Take him to my best customers, have them say nice things, and get through it.

That made sense. But I wanted more. I decided to use Sam's title to open doors I couldn't get through alone.

So, we spent the week driving around Upstate. Sam asked about my life and what I wanted out of this career. I told him we were looking at a house in Rochester and that I wanted to run a business someday.

I scheduled an appointment with Dr. Reed, managing partner of a big surgery center. He held the decision-making power, and I'd never gotten meaningfully through to him. But we were in when I told his assistant that the VP of sales wanted to meet.

When we arrived, Dr. Reed welcomed us, shook our hands, and offered coffee. I'd met him a few times in passing and he remembered me, saying it was good to see me again.

Dr. Reed introduced himself to Sam. Sam leaned in, smiling. "Great to meet you, Dr. Reed. May I call you Ron?" Dr. Reed smiled back. "Of course. And Joel, you can too."

That was something.

Sam and Dr. Reed talked as equals for the next ten minutes, discussing backgrounds and industry shifts. Then Sam led the conversation to their plans for buying new cataract equipment. It wasn't a pitch—it was a business discussion. They went over capital costs, operating costs, value, manufacturing, and the things that make deals last.

Two weeks later, we got the order. But that wasn't the big news.

On the way to the airport, Sam looked at me and said, "Thanks for a great week, Joel. Don't buy that house in Rochester. We're moving you to St. Louis as a product manager. You'll learn to run a business and work with smart people doing the same. I'm asking for two years. You'll probably make less than this year."

"Yes," I said, just like that.

I went home and told my wife we were moving from Buffalo to St. Louis. She just said, "Thank God." I didn't mention the pay cut. It worked out fine.

Sam was right. I took a pay cut, learned to run a business, and worked with people who taught me more than I could have ever imagined.

Mastering Short-Term vs. Long-Term Thinking

Sales is often a high-pressure game, focusing on hitting short-term goals: meeting quotas, closing deals, and driving revenue. While these short-term wins are essential for keeping momentum, they shouldn't be your sole focus. Sales reps who rely entirely on immediate results risk missing out on long-term growth.

Peter Field and Les Binet's 60/40 Rule is an excellent framework for balancing both. They recommend spending 60% of your resources on long-term efforts, like building customer relationships and trust. The other 40% should be focused on short-term wins that meet today's goals. This strategy applies just as well to sales as it does to marketing.

Long-term thinking involves understanding your customer's needs and providing value beyond the immediate sale. If you only focus on short-term tactics like discounts, you become transactional. Customers may come for a deal but won't stay for the relationship. Conversely, reps who invest in relationships build trust and loyalty over time, leading to sustainable success.

As a sales rep aspiring to be a CEO, mastering this balance is essential. CEOs don't just think about this quarter's numbers—they build a vision for future growth. By adopting this mindset, you'll close more deals and position yourself as a leader who understands the bigger picture.

Educating to Create Opportunity and Protect Price

When someone from one healthcare system moves to another, it can mean trouble, especially if they didn't like your rep before. This happened in a system in southern Minnesota. They brought in a new specialist to cut the costs of eye surgery.

Carol came from a big system up in the Twin Cities. She and our sales rep clashed more than once when she had pushed for lower prices. Materials management is a hard job. They're asked to negotiate on products they hardly know.

Sightpath Medical makes it simple. The company provides everything a cataract surgeon needs for surgery—equipment, instruments, supplies, the technician. It's like selling soup—ready to eat.

But when buyers ask about the cost of each ingredient, that's when things get interesting.

Carol called about pricing at a facility where Sightpath already served two surgeons. We knew our job was to help her understand what it costs to deliver everything compared to buying it piece by piece.

So, we focused on educating her, showing that our full service would save her money if they considered all the costs. Once she saw this, she asked if we could look at other facilities in the system where we weren't yet working.

We ran the numbers, showed her the results, and soon after signed a system-wide agreement. It kept our rates steady and doubled our business in the system. Plus, Carol was the hero to her team.

Key Takeaway: The Necessity of Balance

Balancing short-term wins with long-term thinking isn't just smart—it's essential. Focusing too much on the now leaves you vulnerable to losing customers tomorrow, but focusing only on the future means missing out on today's opportunities. The most successful sales reps—and future CEOs—master this balance and build a sales culture around it.

Action Exercises

1. **Short-Term vs. Long-Term Reflection:** Write down one recent sale where you focused on a short-term win and one where you took a long-term relationship-building approach. Reflect on the outcome and how you can apply this balance in future interactions.

2. **Long-Term Strategy Commitment:** Identify one customer where you've been focusing on short-term wins. Over the next month, commit to deepening that relationship through regular communication, offering value beyond your product, and learning about their long-term goals.

3. **60/40 Time Audit:** Track how much of your time this week is spent on short-term activities like closing deals and how much is spent on long-term efforts like relationship-building. Aim to shift your efforts toward a 60/40 balance over the next quarter.

10

From a Single Sale to Achieving Scale: Changing Systems and Processes

You've seen it before: The sales rep who relies on luck, chasing deals without a clear plan and burning out before they hit their quota. That's not you. You want more than a fleeting victory— you want lasting results. In this chapter, you'll learn how to build simple systems and processes that create consistency, free your mind for more significant opportunities, and set you apart as a professional ready to lead.

Building the System, Answering the Question

As a sales professional or manager, you might find yourself in a similar situation. You're part of a team, and you understand the importance of a well-functioning system. You've probably encountered challenges with the tools and processes in place, and you're eager to find a solution that works for everyone.

At Sightpath the core of our operations was a clunky, off-the-shelf version of Microsoft Dynamics. The sales team avoided it, and operations didn't engage with it. It was a patchwork tool without purpose. For a business aiming to scale, we needed more than software. We needed a system that could unite sales, operations, and leadership with shared, accurate visibility into our performance.

We began searching for a new CRM, with Salesforce emerging as the frontrunner. It had the potential to be the backbone of what we were trying to build: A system of processes and accountability that would carry us into the future.

But as we dug into the details, the cracks in our foundation became glaringly obvious.

The Salesforce team engaged us enthusiastically, asking thoughtful questions about our business and goals. Yet one request kept coming up: "Describe your sales process."

At first, it seemed like a routine inquiry. The second time, I wondered if the Salesforce teams were talking to one another. By the fourth, I was pacing up and down a Boston hotel room, holding my phone in one hand and my head in the other.

"This is the fourth time I've been asked to do this exercise," I snapped. "Aren't you guys a CRM company? Shouldn't someone have this written down in our account record by now?"

The line went silent. I knew I'd gone too far. Still, I repeated the explanation for the fourth time, frustration seeping into my words.

That evening, I couldn't let it go on the flight home. I'd spent years pushing for better tools and processes, yet I realized we were missing something fundamental. We weren't building a system—we were patching problems. The sales process we were trying to document didn't truly exist in any unified way. The significance of the "fourth question" became clear to me. It wasn't just a routine inquiry; it was a wake-up call, a realization that we needed to define our sales process before we could build a system around it.

Somewhere over the Midwest, I grabbed a pen and began writing. Step by step, I pieced together what our sales process should look like. It wasn't perfect, but it was a start. I emailed the sales team for feedback, sent the revised version to the Salesforce team, and apologized for my earlier outburst.

Their response was unexpected and eye-opening.

"We keep asking that question," they said, "until someone produces a guiding document. Without it, the process varies from person to person, which makes building the system take longer and much more expensive. It's not about us. It's about you."

It hit me like a thunderbolt: We couldn't build systems and processes without first understanding them ourselves.

Choosing Salesforce was only part of the solution. The real work began when we committed to building a system, not just adopting a tool. The sales process document became our north star, guiding how we tailored the platform to fit our business. We collaborated, aligning sales, operations, and IT around shared goals and workflows.

Adoption didn't happen overnight. It took relentless coaching, unwavering commitment, and a lot of follow-ups to get the team on board. But as the system took shape, so did the results. Salesforce evolved from a piece of software into the backbone of Sightpath's commercial operations.

What began as a frustrating series of questions became the foundation for transformation. Building a system isn't about having the right tools—it's about clarity, alignment, and the willingness to confront your own gaps. Sometimes it takes the fourth question to show you the way forward.

Why Systems Make Sales Sustainable

Every great sales career runs on systems. Systems keep you from forgetting the follow-up call, skipping steps, or letting a golden opportunity slip through the cracks. The most successful sales reps don't wing it. They follow a plan.

Imagine your sales territory as a machine. Without the right parts, it sputters and fails. A strong system is like a well-oiled engine—it doesn't just move; it moves with purpose.

Start small. Build a system for tracking leads. Maybe it's a simple spreadsheet or a CRM tool. Use it every day. Input the names, dates, and notes after each interaction. Don't trust your memory. A system remembers when you don't.

Next, create a process for managing your pipeline. Break it into stages: lead, prospect, opportunity, and close. Each stage has its actions. Know where every deal sits, what's next, and how long it'll take. Review this pipeline weekly. Make adjustments where things slow down.

Another essential system is time management. Block time for specific tasks—calls, emails, prospecting, admin work. Avoid multitasking. Focus fully on one thing at a time. It feels slower but gets more done.

Systems aren't just about efficiency; they're about freedom. Once you trust your systems, your brain stops spinning on small details. That mental clarity opens space for creativity, strategy, and real problem-solving.

When it's time to grow, your systems grow with you. New reps join the team, and you hand them your playbook. They follow what you built. That's leadership. You're not just running a territory; you're building something bigger.

A sales rep with strong systems doesn't just hit their numbers—they understand how to improve them. They see trends, fix bottlenecks, and build for the future. Those are the reps who make it to the CEO's chair.

The Price of Clarity

The pricing process at Sightpath Medical was a delicate balancing act. Each deal was as unique as a snowflake—tailored to the surgeon's needs, location, and requirements. But creating those quotes was messy, ad hoc, and often unreliable. Sales would gather bits of information, operations would patch the gaps, and finance would calculate a price per case.

The system worked—until it didn't.

Too often, assumptions filled the cracks left by incomplete data. Pricing errors led to friction with new customers or delays that jeopardized deals. Worse, there was no reliable way to review how pricing decisions were being made. Every misstep cost time, trust, and money.

Something had to change.

In early 2017, we decided to fix it. We formed the Pricing Committee, a small group that included me, the VP of operations, and our CFO. We outlined a vision: Create a process that delivers accurate, profitable, and scalable deal quotes. It needed to be repeatable and reviewable, a system we could trust as the backbone of our growing business.

But turning that vision into reality wasn't easy.

At first, the process was painfully slow. Sales reps grumbled as deals bogged down, waiting for approvals. Operations needed to provide the level of detail we required. Frustration grew, and so did the temptation to abandon the new system.

Still, we pressed on.

We gave clear feedback to sales and operations about the data we needed to move faster. Slowly, they adapted. Then came the break-through—inviting the operations general managers from each region to join the committee. They became responsible for ensuring the accuracy and completeness of deal information before it reached us.

That change turned the tide.

The results were transformative. With everyone aligned and accountability in place, the pricing process became smooth and efficient. Sales cycles compressed. Reps no longer had to wait for answers; they trusted the system to deliver timely, accurate quotes.

Even better, we now had a central repository—a living history of every deal, decision, and lesson learned. It wasn't just a pricing process anymore; it was the foundation of how we built and scaled our business.

The snowflakes were still unique, but now they fitted into a system that worked. Clarity replaced chaos, trust replaced frustration, and the business thrived because of it.

Key Takeaway: Systems Create Success by Bringing Clarity to Chaos

Systems are the secret to turning chaos into control. They aren't about complexity—they're about consistency. Build them, trust them, and watch as they transform your career from good to great.

Action Exercises

1. **Set Up a System:** Create a system for tracking your leads. Keep it simple and use it every day for the next month.

2. **Break Stages into Actions:** Break your pipeline into at least three stages and list the actions needed for each stage.

3. **Allocate Actions to Time:** Time-block your calendar for one week, assigning specific tasks to specific blocks, and stick to it.

PART FOUR

Understanding Finance, Pricing, and Marketing

As you move from sales rep to CEO, the next critical step is expanding your understanding beyond your own role. The chapters in Part Four will focus on two key areas that are essential to effective leadership: finance and marketing. Understanding how these functions drive the business is crucial to making informed decisions that support growth and sustainability.

Additionally, a strong grasp of pricing strategies will enable you to align your sales efforts with your company's financial goals, ensuring that every deal is not just a win in the short term but contributes to long-term profitability.

As you deepen your knowledge of the broader organization, you'll be better equipped to make strategic decisions that integrate all aspects of the business, moving you closer to the holistic mindset required of a successful CEO.

11

What Makes the World Go Round: Learning the Language of Finance

Most sales reps don't think of themselves as financial experts. Numbers live in a different world—one for accountants, CFOs, and analysts. But here's the truth: The key to earning trust, solving real business problems, and closing bigger deals lies in understanding the language of finance. This chapter will show you how mastering basic financial terms can transform the way you sell, making you a trusted advisor who speaks the language of decision-makers and helping you along the road to the CEO's office.

Sharper Sales: The Blade That Cut Through Obstacles

When I started in sales, I came armed with a biochemistry degree and a knack for science. Numbers didn't scare me, but finance was a foreign language. Selling ophthalmic surgical supplies put me on a steep learning curve, especially when understanding the split between operating and capital expenses—a distinction I didn't initially grasp.

It wasn't just theoretical. This knowledge gap had real stakes. My products included diamond knives and disposable blades used by ophthalmic surgeons during cataract surgeries. Diamond knives, while superior in performance, were considered too expensive by many facilities. Disposable blades, however, won favor with the operating room staff because they were easy to use and budget-friendly. The tension between these perspectives was my battleground.

The surgeons loved the precision of the diamond knives. They swore by their results, calling them indispensable. But the operating room personnel hated them. Diamond knives required careful handling and routine maintenance, which they viewed as extra work. Then there was the financial side: Disposable blades fell under operating expenses—recurring costs that didn't require much approval.

Diamond knives, a higher-ticket item, were classified as capital expenses and needed additional budgetary approval.

Every conversation seemed to hit a wall. The surgeons didn't want to settle for disposable blades, and the staff didn't want the headaches of diamond knife care. Meanwhile, I stood there, trying to bridge the gap with half-formed arguments.

One day, it clicked. What if I leaned into the language of finance? Instead of selling the product, I'd sell the solution in terms their budgets could embrace. I began studying the nuances of operating versus capital expenses, learning how these decisions impacted everyone involved.

I returned to the facilities with this new perspective and shifted my pitch. For the surgeons, I framed the diamond knives as a capital investment in patient outcomes and surgical precision. For the operating room staff, I highlighted how these tools, when properly cared for, reduced operating expenses in the long run. I didn't just sell a product—I offered to train their teams on the care and handling of the knives, easing their concerns and fostering trust.

The result? Surgeons got the tools they needed, the staff felt supported, and the facilities saw financial value in the solution. More importantly, I gained a reputation—not as a product pusher, but as a problem solver.

That experience taught me more than how to sell. It showed me how the correct language and approach could cut through resistance, just like diamond knives.

Why Finance Matters to Sales Reps

Selling is about more than features and benefits—it's about solving problems that matter to your customers. And in business, nothing matters more than money. Every purchase, big or small, comes down to finances. You gain an edge over the competition when you understand how businesses think about revenue, costs, and profitability.

Imagine sitting across from a hospital administrator considering your medical device. They're not just looking at the price tag. They're considering whether this device will attract more patients, increase the efficiency of their operations, and ultimately boost their bottom line.

You'll be more persuasive and credible if you can speak their language—revenue, ROI, and cash flow.

Revenue: More Than Just Sales

Revenue is where it all starts. It's the total income a business earns from its products or services. For your customer, it's their lifeblood. A clinic buying your surgical tool wants to know if it will help them perform more procedures or increase the value of each one. Frame your product as a revenue generator, and you're no longer just selling—you're building their business.

Profit Margins: Where the Money Is Made

Revenue is only part of the story. What matters even more is what's left after costs—the profit margin. If your product helps a business reduce operating costs or increase efficiency, you're directly improving their profit margins. Learn to ask questions like, "How do you measure success for your business?" to uncover what matters most to your customer.

ROI: The Decision-Maker's Litmus Test

Return on investment (ROI) is the "so what" of finance. It answers the question, "If we spend money on this, what do we get back?" Knowing how to calculate and communicate ROI shows you think like a business partner, not just a vendor. For example, "This device costs $50,000, but it typically delivers a 30% ROI within six months" can turn a skeptical buyer into a confident one.

Cash Flow: Timing Is Everything

Cash flow is the pulse of any business. Even if your product offers great ROI, customers might hesitate if they're strapped for cash. Understanding their cash flow challenges allows you to provide creative solutions, like flexible payment terms, to ease their concerns.

The more fluent you are in these financial concepts, the more credible you become. You're not just a rep trying to hit quota; you're the kind of person decision-makers want to work with. They'll see you as a partner, and you will have gained a skill you'll need as you work toward the corner office.

The Year We Stopped Advertising

The national sales meeting buzzed with the usual mix of energy and skepticism. As the sales and marketing leader, I stood before the team, running through the budget for the year. The PowerPoint slide on marketing expenditures had barely flashed onto the screen when a voice from the back interrupted.

"We're not spending anything on marketing this year. Why is that?" The question landed like a stone in the room, halting the quiet hum of side conversations. Heads turned toward me, waiting.

I paused, taking a moment to assess the faces staring back at me. The room was filled with sales reps who had grown accustomed to the high-visibility campaigns of recent years— advertisements in glossy trade magazines, flashy booths at national conventions, and events that turned heads. This was their reality; to them, "marketing" was loud, visible, and exciting. But this year's budget told a different story.

The truth was, we had just come off a two-year blitz for a product launch that had stretched the company's resources. We'd leaned heavily into advertising and events, pushing our limits to make the launch successful. But that pace wasn't sustainable. Now we needed to focus on efficiency and long-term growth, reallocating resources to where they mattered most. That meant scaling back the kind of marketing that made a splash but doubling down on what drove results: direct selling.

I couldn't let the silence stretch too long. The team needed an answer— not just to the question but to the unspoken concern behind it. Was the company losing its way? Were their tools being taken away?

"That's a fair question," I said, stepping away from the podium and folding my arms to signal I wasn't hiding behind slides. "Let me explain."

I reminded them of the new sales compensation plan we recently introduced. It was a win for the team, one that aligned incentives with growth and rewarded their hard work. "That plan," I said, "is a significant investment in you—our sales team. It's not just a line item. It's the most important part of our marketing strategy."

I could see some brows furrow, so I pressed on. "Marketing isn't just about ads or events. It's about how we connect with and keep customers. When we allocate resources, we're making strategic choices. Advertising and events might be cut this year, but we're still investing heavily in what matters most: the direct connection between you and your customers. That's our biggest marketing spend."

Slowly, heads nodded. I explained how these decisions appeared on the profit and loss statement. Advertising, events, and sales compensation were all parts of the broader marketing category, but not all had equal impact.

By the time I finished, the tension in the room had dissipated. They understood that marketing wasn't gone—it had just shifted focus. And, more importantly, they saw themselves as central to the company's strategy.

After the meeting, the same sales rep who'd thrown the tough question my way approached me. "I didn't realize how all that fit together," she said. "Thanks for explaining it." I smiled, knowing a quiet truth: Leadership isn't about avoiding hard questions. It's about meeting them head-on—and using them to help your team see the bigger picture.

Key Takeaway: Call It What They Care About

Speaking the language of finance isn't just a skill—it's a game-changer. When you can connect your product to revenue, profit margins, ROI, or cash flow, you're no longer just selling—you're solving real problems. Decision-makers value someone who understands their business as deeply as they do. By learning these basics, you'll become more than a sales rep; you'll become their go-to advisor.

Action Exercises

1. **Build Your Knowledge:** Identify three financial terms in this chapter that you're least familiar with—research real-world examples of how they're used in business.

2. **Focus on ROI:** Practice explaining ROI for a product you sell using numbers specific to a customer's business.

3. **Learn from Your Colleagues:** Schedule a meeting with someone from your company's finance department to discuss how they evaluate profitability and ROI.

12

Deepening Your Knowledge: Strengthening Your Connections with Finance

As we have seen, your path to the CEO's office might start where you least expect it—in the finance department. Sales reps often overlook this critical connection, focusing instead on customers and quotas. But there's a quiet power in understanding the numbers behind the business. In this chapter, you'll discover why befriending someone in finance could transform your career, how to make that connection, and how it equips you to think and act like a leader.

The Balance of Credits and Debits

It was quarterly review time at Storz Ophthalmics and the buzz in the room was, if anything, even stronger than usual. Financial projections and performance metrics flashed across the screen, with executives around the table analyzing every detail. But as I scanned the numbers, I felt a knot of confusion tighten in my stomach. My team had just achieved a major milestone—$3 million in sales for our new refractive surgery diamond knives. Yet there it was, listed as a *credit*.

I'd always considered sales the lifeblood of the business, the fuel that powered growth. But here, it felt like just a number, something abstract. Why were our successes framed as credits?

As I stared at the financial report, trying to piece it together, Matt Walsh, the finance manager for our surgical division, noticed my furrowed brow. After the meeting, as people filed out of the room, he waved me over with a knowing smile. "Come by my office," he said. "I think I can clear up your confusion."

Cracking the Code

Matt's office felt like stepping into another world—charts covered the walls and spreadsheets glowed on his dual monitors. I sat down, still feeling out of my depth. Finance wasn't my realm. I belonged in the operating room, where instruments hummed, lasers fired, and patients regained their vision.

Matt leaned back in his chair, his tone easy and confident. "You're wondering about those credits, aren't you?"

I nodded, my curiosity outweighing my unease. "It just doesn't make sense. We sell the product—shouldn't that be recorded as a gain? It feels... backward."

He chuckled and picked up a marker, sketching a simple T-account on the whiteboard. "Let me break it down for you. Imagine we sell one of our refractive surgery systems to a surgical center for $50,000. Two things happen. First, our receivables grow by $50,000. That's a debit— value coming in. But where did that value come from? The sale itself."

He pointed to the other side of the T-account. "That's the credit. It's not just a number— it's the story of where the value originated. Every credit shows the source of the value we've captured. Think of it like surgery— every action has an equal and opposite reaction. Perfect balance."

I stared at the board, trying to make the connection. "So, credits are like the starting point? The spark that sets everything in motion?"

"Exactly," he said, grabbing a surgical instrument package from his desk. "Take this. When it was just raw material in our Manchester plant, it was a debit—a use of resources. But it became a credit when it transformed into this precision tool and sold to a surgeon. The source of new value."

That analogy clicked. My clinical background suddenly bridged the gap. "It's like maintaining balance in the anterior chamber during surgery. Every action needs its counterbalance. Otherwise, chaos takes over."

Matt grinned, tapping the whiteboard. "You've got it. In finance, balance isn't just a theory—it's law. And those credits? They're the story of how we create and capture value."

A New Perspective

That conversation changed the way I saw the business. From that day forward, sales reports weren't just numbers on a page. Each credit represented something real: Surgeons trusting our tools, patients regaining their vision, and lives improved because of our work.

During a team dinner at the next national sales meeting, I raised my glass and caught Matt's eye. "Here's to credits," I said with a grin.

Matt beamed like a proud teacher. It wasn't just about debits and credits anymore—it was about understanding the bigger picture. Balance wasn't only for the books or the operating room. It was the foundation for everything in business and life.

Seeing Beyond Sales: Why Finance Matters

At first, it might seem like finance and sales operate in different worlds. One team crunches numbers; the other drives revenue. But these worlds are deeply intertwined. Sales is the engine, and finance ensures the fuel keeps flowing. Without understanding this relationship, your decisions might serve only short-term goals, leaving long-term opportunities untapped.

Your finance colleagues aren't just number crunchers; they're strategic advisors. They can help you understand how your sales affect company profitability, how payment terms shape cash flow, and what financial trends signal about market health. Think of finance as the company's control tower, offering a clear view of what's ahead.

Finding Your Finance Ally and Building the Connection

The first step is to find the right person. Larger companies often have teams focused on different aspects of finance, such as accounts receivable, financial planning and analysis (FP&A), or corporate finance. Start small—ask questions that reveal their expertise, like how a customer's payment history might influence sales decisions.

In smaller organizations where finance teams wear multiple hats, your ally may have an even broader understanding of the company's operations. These roles offer a unique opportunity for sales reps to gain a 360-degree view of the business.

Be Curious, Not Transactional

Approach finance with genuine curiosity. Instead of asking for data or approval, ask for insight. Simple, respectful questions like, "How do our payment terms affect cash flow?" or, "What financial trends should I consider when structuring deals?" open the door to collaboration.

Focus on Shared Goals

Both sales and finance care about the company's success. Frame your questions around common objectives. For instance, "How can I structure deals to better support the company's financial goals?" shows you're thinking strategically.

Add Value Where You Can

You might think you have little to offer, but your front-line knowledge is gold to finance. Sharing customer insights—like delayed payments or unexpected hurdles—can help them manage the business more effectively.

Stay Transparent

If a deal is at risk or a customer's payment behavior changes, don't keep it to yourself. Finance values honesty. A trust-based relationship creates mutual respect and positions you as a reliable partner.

The Benefits of Financial Literacy

Understanding finance doesn't just improve your sales. It gives you a CEO's perspective. You start thinking about margins, cash flow, and long-term strategy. These insights make you a better sales rep and prepare you for leadership.

By learning from finance, you'll speak the language of decision-makers. Customers will trust your advice more, and executives will see your potential. The result? You're no longer just a sales rep—you're a trusted business partner with the tools to lead.

Thrown Out to Win: Lessons from a Hospital Basement

It was late on a Thursday afternoon. I was driving home from Rochester, New York, to Orchard Park, enjoying the changing shades of the sunset across the sky. The phone rang. Jenny from accounts receivable was on the line. Her voice was steady but tinged with frustration.

"Joel, I need your help," she said. "Medina Memorial Hospital's materials manager, Chuck, refuses to pay their past-due bill. He says the pricing is wrong, but it's not. Any chance you can do something?"

I glanced at the exit sign for Medina, just a few miles up the road. "I'm passing by right now," I replied. "I'll stop in and talk to him."

I pulled into the hospital parking lot, already sensing this wouldn't be a straightforward visit. Materials management offices were often in the basement, tucked away like secrets no one wanted to share. I made my way down the dim hallway and was ushered into Chuck's office.

Chuck was direct and without pleasantries. "We're not paying that bill. Your pricing is higher than Ioptex, and we're not paying more."

I calmly slid a copy of the contract across his desk. "Here's the pricing you agreed to," I said. "It reflects the added value of having these implants ready for emergency cases. What am I missing?"

Chuck's face tightened. "I don't care what the contract says. I'm not paying more than Ioptex's price."

I explained the importance of having our implants available for those rare cases that required suturing into the eye, but Chuck wasn't budging. Each round of conversation ended in the same place: "I'm not paying."

I could feel my frustration mounting. Finally, with a touch of sarcasm, I said, "Unfortunately, Chuck, you signed that contract, and Ioptex doesn't set our prices."

His face flushed with anger. He pointed to the door. "Get out of my hospital."

I left, the weight of the confrontation settling in. Ten minutes later, my phone rang again as I merged back onto the Thruway. This time, it was Dr. Mruchuck, the hospital's lead cataract surgeon. His voice was measured but firm.

"Joel, you've crossed a line. You should have scheduled an appointment and handled yourself more professionally. Don't come back here unannounced."

I started to explain, but he cut me off. "This conversation is over," he said before hanging up.

The following week, a letter arrived at our corporate office, addressed to the vice president of sales and marketing, Sam Alioto. It was from Dr. Mruchuck, and it wasn't a glowing review of my performance. The words "unprofessional" and "disruptive" jumped off the page, and my stomach sank.

But then I saw Sam's handwritten note at the bottom: "Keep fighting for our business, Joel. If you never get thrown out of a hospital, you're not making things happen!"

I smiled. Chuck paid the bill. Over the next few months, I rebuilt my relationship with Dr. Mruchuck. I scheduled appointments and kept my tone professional. Slowly but surely, I won him over. He became a loyal customer, and Medina Memorial became an account we could count on.

It wasn't the smoothest path, but it reminded me of a truth I'd come to live by: Relationships, persistence, and even a few missteps are all part of the process. Jenny from accounts receivable had called me because she knew I'd go to bat for her. In the end, that trust made all the difference.

Key Takeaway: Think Bigger, Act Smarter

Making a friend in finance is about more than understanding numbers. It's about expanding your perspective and sharpening your skills. When you connect with finance, you gain a mentor who teaches you to see beyond the monthly sales targets. That vision sets you apart. That vision builds careers.

Action Exercises

1. **Map the Finance Department:** Identify roles in your company's finance team. List their responsibilities and consider who might be the best resource for you.

2. **Start a Conversation:** Schedule a meeting with someone in finance. Prepare three thoughtful questions about how sales and finance intersect.

3. **Analyze a Deal:** Review a recent deal with financial metrics in mind. Seek feedback from finance to understand its broader impact on the company.

13

From Financial Fluency to Pricing Profit: Why Pricing Is Leadership

You don't have to be in the boardroom to start thinking like a CEO. Every time you negotiate pricing, you make decisions shaping your business's future. This chapter will show you how mastering pricing strategy as a sales rep sets the stage for leadership, builds trust with your team, and gives you the skills to one day run the company.

Thinking Fast Under Pressure

The Calm Before the Storm

Selling intraocular lens implants (IOLs) was rewarding but demanding work. One day, I got a call from Charles, the materials manager at a hospital that used our products. Charles wasn't the type to make small talk, so I knew something was brewing when he invited me to meet.

He greeted me with a huge smile, a stark departure from his typical no-nonsense demeanor. As I followed him into his office, my instincts told me this wasn't a casual conversation. I was right.

Charles placed a letter from his group purchasing organization (GPO) on his desk with a dramatic flourish. "Take a look," he said, grinning.

A Deal Too Good to Beat

The letter was terrible news. It stated that the GPO had signed a new agreement with the manufacturer of a product we sold. They offered the same product we sold for $150 at a drastically reduced price of $100.

Charles leaned back in his chair, relishing the moment. "It says here that all distributors will adjust pricing immediately," he declared, his grin now razor-sharp.

This wasn't just a threat to my deal—it was a 33% price cut on a product we relied on for profitability. My stomach tightened, but I didn't let it show. I needed a solution—and fast.

Turning the Tables

I kept my tone steady. "Great, Charles. We'll match that for the IOL," I said. "But what does the letter say about the injector for the IOL?"

Charles blinked. "The injector? Nothing," he replied, suddenly less sure of his advantage.

I leaned in. "That's because the $150 bundle you're used to includes both the IOL and the injector—$100 for the lens and $50 for the injector. If you'd like, we can invoice them separately."

The grin faded from Charles's face as he realized his leverage had evaporated. "I didn't know about your pricing structure," he muttered, visibly deflated.

My quick thinking saved the account and maintained our pricing integrity. While others might have folded to the GPO's demands, I turned the situation around by staying calm and looking beyond the obvious.

Creativity Beats Conformity

Moments like these define the journey from sales rep to CEO. It's not just about selling a product; it's about seeing the bigger picture, adapting quickly, and finding solutions no one else sees. Challenges, even when they seem impossible, are just opportunities waiting for a fresh perspective.

Pricing as a Cornerstone of Leadership

To most sales reps, pricing feels like a hurdle. To a future CEO, it's a tool. When you manage pricing wisely, you show that you understand more than just sales—you understand business. Every pricing decision sends a ripple through the company, impacting revenue, profitability, and even brand perception. Learning to manage those ripples sets you apart.

Start with this: Pricing is never just about the customer. It's also about what you communicate internally. When you hold the line on pricing, you show leadership that you're focused on value, not quick wins. This builds trust, proving that you're not just chasing numbers—you're protecting the company's long-term health.

Think about what happens when you discount too often. The business makes less money, which lowers margins and impacts funding for other departments. Operations might get squeezed, marketing budgets shrink, and research and development lose critical resources. A rep who consistently discounts shows they're thinking small—about one sale instead of the entire system.

On the other hand, a rep who confidently defends pricing demonstrates vision. They understand that every dollar matters, not just to their paycheck but to the company's future. This mindset is what separates a good sales rep from a future CEO.

Learning to manage pricing also teaches you negotiation and strategy—skills every CEO needs. When you stand firm on value, you're not just selling a product; you're persuading others to see the worth in what you offer. This is the same skill you'll use as a leader to rally teams, secure funding, and build a vision for the company.

Finally, managing pricing teaches you to think about profit. CEOs don't just drive revenue—they ensure the company thrives financially. As a sales rep, you can begin practicing this by understanding how your pricing decisions affect the bottom line. Ask questions: What's our margin? How does discounting affect profitability? When you approach pricing this way, you're stepping into the shoes of a leader.

The Cost of Compromise: A Lesson in Value at Sightpath Medical

A CFO's Breaking Point

The CFO sat in his office, besieged by numbers and decisions. Stacks of reports cluttered his desk, each detailing another price reduction pushed by the sales team. The CFO of Sightpath Medical, had always prided himself on financial discipline. Yet here he was, being asked to sign off on deals that gnawed away at the company's margins.

The requests came steadily: lower pricing for existing customers, discounts for new ones, and a relentless tide of compromise. The sales reps argued these cuts were necessary to stay competitive. But to the CFO, they were a slow bleed. His patience was running out. He slammed his pen down one afternoon and called me.

"Joel," he said, his tone clipped. "We're giving away the store. If this keeps up, there won't be a company left to sell for."

Bridging Two Worlds

I understood the CFO's frustration. As the head of sales and marketing, I wanted growth, but not at the expense of sustainability. We had a problem—sales reps often believed that lowering prices was the only lever to close a deal. What they didn't grasp was the ripple effect. Each price cut undermined the company's long-term health, devalued our offerings, and set a dangerous precedent with customers.

The CFO and I had to find common ground. It wasn't enough to veto discounts; we needed the team to understand why this approach was unsustainable. Together, we crafted a plan—a series of conversations and training sessions to educate the sales team on the financial realities of discounting.

In one meeting, the CFO brought the raw data: Charts showing how even a small percentage reduction in pricing impacted profitability. I added stories from the field, recounting how competitors who slashed prices struggled to survive. We emphasized the importance of selling value, not just cost.

The sessions were not without resistance. Some reps pushed back, insisting that price was the only deciding factor for customers. Others simply nodded, unconvinced. The CFO, usually reserved, became the unlikely hero of these meetings, delivering plainspoken truths that cut through the noise.

Selling Value Over Price

Weeks turned into months, and the shift was gradual but tangible. The sales team began leaning into value-based selling, focusing on the unique benefits Sightpath brought to its customers. They learned to ask better questions, uncover customer pain points, and position our solutions as worth the investment.

The CFO noticed the difference first. The frequency of discount requests dropped, replaced by more strategic deal structures. One afternoon, he walked into my office with a rare grin.

"It's working," he said. "We're holding the line, and the numbers are backing it up."

The results spoke for themselves. Revenue stabilized, and the company gained a reputation for standing by its value. More importantly, we built a culture of respect—for our product, our customers, and the work it took to deliver excellence.

The CFO's resolve and our collaboration had saved Sightpath from the dangerous spiral of endless discounting. It wasn't just about margins; it was about preserving the integrity of the business.

Key Takeaway: Pricing Is Power

Managing prices isn't just about closing deals—it's about stepping into a leadership mindset. When you master pricing, you prove that you can think strategically, defend value, and make decisions that strengthen the company. These are the skills that pave the way from sales rep to CEO.

Action Exercises

1. **Analyze the Numbers:** Work with your finance team to understand how pricing impacts profitability. Create a simple chart showing how discounts affect margins.

2. **Role-Play Leadership Scenarios:** Practice responding to customers who push for discounts. Focus on demonstrating value and staying firm.

3. **Track Your Pricing Strategy:** Keep a journal of your pricing decisions for one month. Note how they impact relationships, revenue, and your confidence.

14

Allies on the Journey: The Magic of Marketing

Sales and marketing often feel like rival teams playing the same game. But the truth is, when these two departments work together, magic happens. As a sales rep, forming a solid bond with marketing can unlock insights about your market, refine your pitch, and boost your numbers. This chapter shows you how to make a marketing ally and why that relationship is crucial for sales success and your path to leadership.

The Diamond Edge of Influence

Being a marketing product manager is challenging. You carry the weight of hitting a number but have no direct authority to command anyone to do the work. It's a tightrope walk where success hinges on influence rather than control. Back when I was a sales rep, I saw this dynamic up close and learned how valuable it could be to have a strong ally in marketing.

At national sales meetings, I made it a point to connect with the marketing product managers. These were the people who owned the product lines I needed to improve. They were gatekeepers to the expertise I lacked.

Among them was Blake Michaels, the product manager for surgical instruments, including the diamond knives used in refractive surgery.

Selling diamond knives was no simple feat. At the time, refractive surgery wasn't laser based as it is now. Instead, surgeons relied on precision-crafted diamond knives to reshape the cornea. These tools weren't just sharp; they were intricate, and selling them meant understanding every nuance of their design and application. One slip in knowledge could cost a sale or erode trust with a surgeon.

Blake was my lifeline. Whenever I had a question, he'd take the time to walk me through the details. He didn't just tell me what to say—he made sure I understood why one knife model outperformed another. I'll never forget the time I struggled with a pitch for a knife that a surgeon was skeptical about. Blake explained how its unique blade shape could unintentionally plow through tissue if misused, affecting surgical outcomes. That insight gave me the edge I needed to guide the surgeon toward a better option—and win the sale.

But Blake wasn't just technically sharp; he was always patient and available. This stood out to me because not every product manager was like that. Some kept their distance, guarding their expertise like a secret. Not Blake. He treated me like a partner, not just a rep looking for a quick fix.

Years later, I found myself in Blake's shoes. I became the instrument product manager. Suddenly, I was the one juggling the responsibility of driving results without the authority to demand action. And in those moments, I remembered Blake. His willingness to share his expertise, his patience, his consistency—it all came rushing back.

I made a choice. I wouldn't hoard knowledge or see sales reps as interruptions. Like Blake, I'd make myself available. I'd help reps sharpen their pitch, find new angles, and close deals. Influence wasn't about authority; it was about service. Blake had shown me that. Now it was my turn to pass it on.

Finding Gold in the Marketing Department

Marketing is often seen as the backstage crew, but they're the ones setting the stage for your performance. They build awareness, create demand, and nurture leads before they land in your hands. A good marketing partner can amplify your efforts, giving you the edge to close deals faster and more effectively.

Why You Need Marketing

As a sales rep, you know firsthand customer pain points and objections. But marketing has something you don't: a bird's-eye view of the market. They analyze trends, map out buyer behaviors, and create content that speaks to your audience before you ever step into the conversation. Think of marketing as the strategist and you as the tactician. Together, you're unstoppable.

If you've ever struggled to find the right messaging or felt like your leads weren't qualified, marketing is your go-to partner. They can help you understand the customer journey, provide insights into your ideal customer profiles, and share tools like email templates or case studies that resonate with prospects. The key is building a relationship that turns insights into action.

Shifting Your Mindset: Marketing as a Profit and Loss Driver

Many reps don't realize they're part of the marketing budget. As a CEO might say, "Sales is marketing in action." Your salary, travel expenses, and commissions are all part of the marketing spend on the company's profit and loss statement. This perspective changes everything. Instead of viewing marketing as a separate entity, you start seeing yourself as their frontline representative.

This mindset shift is critical. It helps you understand that sales and marketing aren't competing—they're complementary. A unified strategy means every marketing dollar spent is more likely to convert into revenue. When you collaborate with marketing, you're not just boosting your territory's performance—you're strengthening the company's financial health.

Building the Relationship

Finding the right person in marketing can feel like finding a needle in a haystack, especially in large organizations. Look for someone who regularly interacts with sales—like a product marketing manager or a digital strategist. In smaller companies, you might work directly with the person creating campaigns and running analytics.

Start small. Schedule a casual meeting to learn about their work. Ask how they build personas, what tools they use, and how they think sales could be more effective. Share your insights from the field—customer objections, common challenges, and feedback on recent campaigns. The more you give, the more they'll invest in helping you.

Collaboration takes effort. Join marketing calls when possible, and don't be afraid to contribute. Suggest pilot programs for your territory or offer to test new messaging. These small steps show you're invested in their success, and in turn, they'll be invested in yours.

How This Alliance Grows Your Career

A marketing ally does more than help you hit quota. They teach you how the business works. By understanding campaigns, analytics, and customer journeys, you start thinking strategically—like a leader. CEOs need to know how to align departments and drive results. Your work with marketing prepares you for that responsibility.

The Bridge Builder

Balancing the needs of sales and marketing is like refereeing a sibling rivalry. Each department wants the other to understand its perspective, but neither feels genuinely heard. As the leader of both departments at

Sightpath Medical, I often found myself in the middle, trying to broker peace. Sales wanted tools they claimed would help close deals, while marketing felt sales didn't use what they had already created. It was a perpetual cycle of frustration.

Then there was Jeffrey Martin, our director of content marketing. Unlike others, Jeffrey wasn't just about pushing ideas from behind a desk. He understood something many didn't: Success comes from listening. And he was very good at it.

It was late 2016, and we were preparing our marketing plan for the coming year. I tasked Jeffrey with something different: meet with every sales rep individually. "Ask them what they need to succeed next year," I said. Jeffrey nodded, eager to dive in.

Weeks passed, and Jeffrey came back with his findings. The results were surprising. Each rep wanted something completely different. One needed more detailed brochures for surgeons, another asked for digital presentations tailored to hospitals, and someone else wanted localized data sheets. The needs weren't just varied—they were hyper-specific.

Sitting across from Jeffrey, I sifted through his notes. "This is good," I said, "but how do we act on all this?" Marketing plans weren't supposed to get this granular. I hesitated before asking, "Could we take marketing down to the territory level?"

Jeffrey leaned back, his brow furrowed in thought. He was a "can-do" kind of person, but this was a big ask. Custom marketing for each territory? It sounded daunting. After a moment, he smiled. "Sure. Why not?"

And just like that, Territory-Based Content Marketing was born. Together, Jeffrey and I built a strategy to deliver customized marketing materials for every sales territory. The work wasn't easy, but the results spoke volumes. Sales reps felt heard, and their requests were met with tangible solutions that fitted their unique needs.

Jeffrey's secret wasn't in the strategy itself but in how it started. He built trust by listening and connecting with each rep personally. He didn't just create a plan—he created relationships. That trust became the foundation of our success.

When we rolled out the program in 2017, the sales team didn't just like it—they loved it. For the first time, they felt like true partners with marketing. And all it took was one person willing to build a bridge where none had existed before.

Key Takeaway: Marketing is the Secret Weapon of Sales

The best sales reps are team players who understand that marketing is their secret weapon. When you work together, you create a unified customer experience that drives trust and loyalty. Start building those bridges now, and you'll improve your sales performance and gain a deeper understanding of how to lead and align teams—a skill that will serve you well as a future CEO.

Action Exercises

1. **Reach Out to Marketing:** Identify a marketing professional in your organization. Schedule a meeting to discuss how you can collaborate, share one customer insight you've gathered, and ask for their perspective.

2. **Align Your Sales Pitch:** Review the latest marketing materials. Adjust your pitch to reflect current campaigns or messaging, test the updated pitch with a prospect, and share feedback with marketing.

3. **Learn the Numbers:** Ask your marketing or finance team how direct selling costs are calculated. Discuss how marketing and sales jointly impact profit and loss and reflect on how this understanding changes your approach to sales.

PART FIVE

Understanding the World Around You

As you transition from sales rep to CEO, it's crucial to expand your focus beyond internal operations and develop a deep understanding of the world around your company. This section will emphasize the importance of truly knowing your customers—their needs, behaviors, and pain points—so that you can build solutions that resonate and create lasting value. Alongside this, you'll need to become comfortable with the metrics that define your success, as these numbers will guide your strategic decisions and help you measure progress.

Equally important is understanding content marketing, which has become an essential tool for building brand awareness, engaging customers, and driving growth. As a CEO, your ability to connect with your market through meaningful content will play a key role in establishing your company's presence and fostering long-term relationships.

These steps are vital as you move from focusing solely on individual sales to developing a broader, more strategic view that will drive your company's success.

15

Speaking the Language of Success: Why Metrics Matter

Numbers aren't just numbers—they're the language of success. When you understand them, they tell you where you're winning, where you're losing, and how to fix it. In this chapter, you'll learn how to uncover the truth in your sales key performance indicators (KPIs), improve your performance, and set yourself apart as a leader in the making.

The Metric That Changed Everything for Me

A Data-Driven World

When I began working in sales leadership at a private equity-sponsored company, I discovered how much numbers dictate decisions. Spreadsheets, dashboards, and KPIs weren't just tools—they were lifelines. Private equity firms live and breathe by them.

The pressure was even more intense at Sightpath Medical, where I became vice president of sales. We were seven months into private equity ownership, and our sales and customer data gaps were glaring.

The numbers didn't match up. Discussions with the board of directors were fraught with uncertainty. Everyone wanted answers, but the data rarely gave them. It was a tough environment where curiosity often felt like criticism.

The Question That Stopped Me

One day during a board meeting, a director zeroed in on me. "Joel, what percent of your revenue comes from new customers who have been with you less than a year?" His tone was sharp, his gaze direct.

I glanced at our CFO, hoping for backup. He just shrugged.

I stammered, "We don't track that. We're focused on how we're performing against the plan." My words sounded hollow even to me.

The director's frustration was palpable. He leaned forward and said, "You should start keeping track of that data. It can be a strong indicator of your business's long-term health."

That moment lingered in the air. My instinct was to defend, to explain why we didn't have the data. But I stopped myself. I nodded and said, "Thank you for the insight."

It was a humbling moment. I realized that the director's curiosity wasn't the enemy—my defensiveness was.

A New Favorite Metric

We took the director's advice. Revenue from new customers became a KPI, and tracking it transformed how we saw the business. We published the data by sales territory, revealing a troubling pattern: Reps chased deals but neglected follow-through. No one questioned what came next as long as they hit their quotas.

This simple metric sparked change. Sales reps began to see beyond the numbers on their dashboards. They focused not only on closing deals but on nurturing new customers. With coaching, the team understood the deeper story behind their numbers. Results improved, not just because of quotas but because of sustained growth.

That question—sharp, pointed, and uncomfortable—became a turning point. It taught me to embrace curiosity, even when it stung. It also taught me something bigger: The numbers always tell a story, but only if you're brave enough to ask the right questions.

Metrics don't just measure—they reveal. And sometimes, the right question can change everything.

What to Measure: Sales KPIs That Shape Success

Sales is more than closing deals—it's knowing what works and what doesn't. To get there, you need to track the right KPIs. These numbers don't just measure where you are; they point to where you need to go. Let's break down the six KPIs that will help you understand and transform your sales outcomes.

Quota Attainment

Your quota is your scoreboard, but it's only the surface. Look deeper. If you're overperforming, where's the growth coming from? If you're under, what's slipping through the cracks? Every number has a reason behind it.

Pipeline Velocity

This measures how fast deals move through your pipeline. A slow pipeline shows hesitation—either yours or your prospects. Speed comes from urgency, clear communication, and knowing what to ask for at each stage.

Win Rate

Winning isn't just about closing deals. It's about closing the right ones. If you're chasing leads that rarely convert, it's time to rethink your target list. Quality beats quantity every time.

Sales Cycle Length

How long does it take you to close a deal? Long cycles mean wasted time and missed opportunities. Shorten the cycle, and you'll not only close more—you'll have time to find new prospects.

Customer Lifetime Value (CLTV)

A one-time sale is nice, but a long-term customer pays dividends. CLTV shifts your focus to relationships. The bigger the value, the more they trust you—and the more likely they'll stay.

Revenue from New Customers

Growth doesn't just come from the customers you have—it comes from the ones you don't. Measuring revenue from new customers shows how well you're expanding your reach. It's not just about numbers; it's about ensuring you're connecting with the right prospects and offering real value to bring them on board.

Understanding and Managing Customer Churn Rates

Customer churn rate is one of the most critical Key Performance Indicators (KPIs) for any business. The churn rate refers to the percentage of customers who stop doing business with you over a given period. It's a stark reminder that retaining customers is a constant challenge, no matter how good your products or services are.

Why Churn Rate Matters to Sales Reps

Understanding customer churn is not just a "nice to know" metric for a sales rep aspiring to become CEO—it's essential. High customer churn signals potential problems, such as dissatisfaction with the product or service, unmet expectations, or better offers from competitors. It directly impacts revenue, profitability, and the company's growth trajectory.

Moreover, customer churn is expensive. Acquiring new customers often costs five to seven times more than retaining existing ones. For a sales rep, keeping current customers happy and engaged can be the fastest route to achieving quotas, building strong relationships, and demonstrating leadership potential to the company.

How to Calculate Customer Churn Rate

The formula for churn rate is straightforward:

Churn Rate = (Number of Customers Lost During a Period / Total Customers at the Start of the Period) × 100

For example, if you started the quarter with 1,000 customers and lost 50 by the end, your churn rate for the quarter is:

(50 / 1,000) × 100 = 5%

Understanding this metric is just the beginning. The real value lies in interpreting the number and taking action.

What High Churn Rates Tell You

A high churn rate is a red flag that something in the business isn't working. It could indicate issues such as:

- Poor product performance or quality
- Ineffective customer onboarding or support
- Misaligned customer expectations during the sales process
- Lack of perceived value from your product or service

As a sales rep, this KPI should encourage you to investigate why customers are leaving and how to prevent it. Often, the churn problem starts earlier in the customer journey, during the sales process.

Practical Steps to Reduce Churn

While some churn is inevitable, you can minimize it by focusing on proactive measures. Here are key strategies to consider:

1. **Understand Your Customer's Needs:** Build relationships that go beyond transactions. Knowing your customers' long-term goals lets you position your product as part of their success.

2. **Set Clear Expectations:** Be honest and transparent about what your product can and cannot do. Misaligned expectations often lead to early dissatisfaction.

3. **Ensure Proper Handoffs:** If your role ends after the sale, offer your customer a seamless and trustworthy introduction to their onboarding or support team.

4. **Monitor Customer Health:** Use tools like Net Promoter Scores (NPS) or customer satisfaction surveys to gauge engagement and satisfaction. Watch for early signs of dissatisfaction.

5. **Provide Ongoing Value:** Keep customers informed about new features, updates, and best practices. Demonstrate that your company is committed to their success.

How Churn Rate Connects to Leadership

The ability to analyze churn rates and take corrective actions shows commitment to customers and the company's bottom line. For a sales rep with aspirations of becoming a CEO, this demonstrates a results-driven mindset combined with strategic thinking. CEOs who understand churn rates and their root causes are better equipped to make decisions that drive long-term growth.

When you take the initiative to address churn at the ground level, you position yourself as a problem solver and leader. It's not just about closing the next sale; it's about ensuring the company retains the value of every sale made.

How to Improve Your Metrics

Once you know your KPIs, the work begins. Improving performance takes discipline, curiosity, and a willingness to change. Start small but think big. Improving these key metrics isn't just about working harder—it's about working smarter. Here's how.

Simplify Your Approach

Strip your process down to its core. Ask yourself: What's working? What's not? The answers might surprise you.

Focus on Inputs, Not Just Outputs

Metrics like calls, emails, and meetings matter. But it's not just about numbers—it's about quality. Are your actions driving progress? If not, tweak them.

Learn From Others

Don't be afraid to ask for help. Managers and top performers can offer insights you haven't considered. Watch them. Ask questions. Apply what works for them to your process.

Take Ownership

When something isn't working, own it. Excuses won't get you far. Find the problem, fix it, and keep moving forward.

Wine, Twine, and Wallet Share

The surgeon was a prize customer. He performed most of his surgical volume at a hospital in his hometown—territory I wanted badly. Selling him on using my intraocular lens implants at his satellite surgery locations had been a win, but the real gold lay at that hospital. I just needed a way to tip the scales.

That's when I learned he was an avid wine collector—the kind of enthusiast who scoured lists for elusive bottles. A chance mention of his frustration at being unable to track down certain wines lit a spark. My father-in-law was in the wine business.

Opportunity was knocking.

One afternoon, the surgeon called. He'd been searching for a rare wine to serve at his holiday party—forty-eight bottles. Could I find it?

I called my father-in-law, who located the wine after some work. When I got the price, my stomach sank. It wasn't in my budget—not by a long shot.

I braced myself, picked up the phone, and called the surgeon. I told him I'd found the wine but couldn't afford to pay for it. To my relief, he chuckled and said he never expected me to cover it. He was just thrilled I could track it down. One problem solved.

The next challenge was delivery. The wine had to arrive on time for his party. The surgeon suggested meeting at one of his satellite offices, about 120 miles from me. It seemed simple enough, but there was a twist—my ten-year-old son was home on holiday break and itching for an adventure.

"Want to come with me to see the world's largest ball of twine?" I asked him. He agreed, probably expecting something magical.

We loaded up the wine and hit the road.

The drop-off went smoothly. The surgeon was thrilled; we even stayed for lunch with him and his staff. It felt like a win, but the highlight for my son was still ahead.

We arrived in Dawson, Minnesota, and stood before the world's largest ball of twine. My son stared at it, blinking in disbelief.

"Is that it, Dad?"

His disappointment was palpable. Dairy Queen was nearby, so I salvaged the trip with a Raspberry Malt. As we drove home, I wondered if he'd ever let me live down the twine escapade.

A few weeks later, the phone rang. It was the surgeon's hometown hospital. He'd asked them to switch his implants to mine. Just like that, the deal was done.

All it took was listening to his needs—unrelated to my product—and helping solve a problem. Along the way, I made a memory with my son I'll never forget, which we still joke about today. Sometimes, it's that simple.

Key Takeaway: Stay Ahead by Owning Your Numbers

Your numbers are the story of your success. When you track the right metrics and take disciplined action, you gain control of your performance and your future. Mastering this skill isn't just about hitting quotas—it's about becoming a leader others look up to.

Action Exercises

1. **The Daily Metric Tracker:** Choose one KPI to focus on daily for a month. Track it consistently and analyze what drives changes. Then, share your findings with your manager or team.

2. **Pipeline Audit:** Review your pipeline for stalled opportunities. Identify the common obstacles and create a plan to address them. Then, test different approaches to see what moves deals forward faster.

3. **Customer Value Challenge:** Pick one customer and calculate their CLTV. Brainstorm ways to increase their value through upselling or cross-selling and track your progress over the next three months.

4. **Identify** three customers who stopped doing business with your company in the past quarter. Reach out to them and try to uncover why they left. Share your findings with your manager.

5. **Review** your territory's churn rate over the past year. Look for trends or commonalities among customers who churned and identify one action to address the root cause.

6. **Develop** a post-sale strategy for your accounts with at least three touchpoints to reinforce value and build trust.

16

Unlocking Insights: It's All About Understanding Your Customers

What separates good sales reps from great ones? It's the ability to see what others overlook—to find clarity in the chaos and use those "Aha" moments to drive success. This chapter will show you how to unlock the kind of insight that can transform your sales performance and set you on the path to leadership. By learning to think like your customers and anticipate their needs, you'll develop a skill set that goes beyond sales and prepares you for the executive suite.

Seeing Beyond the Sale: The Persona That Changed the Game

The Narrow View

Sales success often hinges on seeing your customers clearly. But what happens when your view is too narrow? At Sightpath, we thought we had it figured out. We built a robust content marketing strategy based on four customer personas. Each persona was meticulously crafted to target the distinct needs of ophthalmologists, administrators, and other stakeholders.

It worked—at least, we thought it did. The numbers were respectable, and the sales team was hitting their quotas. Yet, there was a nagging question we couldn't ignore: Were we leaving opportunities on the table?

The Blind Spot

Midway through the second year of this strategy, the results plateaued. Our leads weren't growing, and we couldn't pinpoint why. A gut feeling pushed us to reevaluate. Had we missed someone important? As we combed through feedback, a hidden trend emerged: channel partner sales reps.

These reps, who worked for manufacturers, were critical influencers in the buying process. They weren't just connectors; they were decision-makers in their own right, often shaping how and when our products reached end customers.

It became clear—they weren't just a secondary consideration. They were an untapped customer persona. But how could we create content that resonated with them? And, more importantly, would it work?

Expanding the Horizon

We took the leap, adding channel partner sales reps to our persona strategy. With an edge strategy mindset, we built tailored content designed to address their unique challenges and motivations. It wasn't just a tweak but a shift in how we defined our customer universe.

The results were immediate and undeniable. Leads from channel partners spiked. Deals that had once been stuck in limbo started moving. These reps, now armed with tools designed specifically for them, became advocates for our brand.

We transformed a flatlining strategy into a growing success by redefining who our customers were. The experience was a lesson in humility and vision: Never assume you've seen the complete picture. Often, the answers lie just beyond the edges of what you think you know.

The Lesson

In sales, anticipating your customer's needs is more than a skill; it's an art. Sometimes, the best insights come not from looking inward but by expanding outward. That's what separates those who stay sales reps from those who rise to become CEOs.

The Insight Advantage: Thinking Like Your Customer

The secret to becoming indispensable as a sales rep lies in understanding your customer better than anyone else. Too many salespeople focus solely on their product or service, rattling off features without grasping the customer's needs. The truth is that customers don't buy features—they buy solutions to their problems.

Imagine you're pitching to a hospital administrator. You could discuss how your surgical device has a faster setup time than the competition. But what if you knew the administrator's biggest concern wasn't time but avoiding post-surgical complications? Your pitch would shift from faster setup to better patient outcomes, resonating far more deeply.

The first step to gaining this kind of insight is to develop personas. Think of a persona as a detailed sketch of your ideal customer, built from real-world experiences. Start with questions: Who are they? What keeps them awake at night? What do they dream about achieving? Personas aren't just for marketers—they're tools for anyone who wants to sell smarter and build stronger relationships.

Take Alan Cooper's story (told in more detail below) as an example. He was a software developer who revolutionized his field by creating a persona called "Kathy." Instead of obsessing over code, he focused on what Kathy, the end-user, would want. This approach helped him develop software that solved real problems. As a sales rep, you're in the perfect position to create your personas because you interact with customers daily. You gather insights whenever you listen to their frustrations or watch them light up when you hit on a solution.

Once you have a persona, map out the buyer's journey. This is the path your customer takes from identifying a problem to choosing a solution. Knowing this process helps you meet them at the right time with the right message. Are they in the early stages, just realizing they have a problem? Or are they comparing vendors, trying to decide who to trust? By tailoring your approach, you'll close more deals and show your company that you think strategically—an essential trait for any future CEO.

Finally, adapt your approach to generational differences. Millennials, for instance, value authenticity and expect personalization. They don't want to feel like they're being sold to; they want to be understood. Older generations might appreciate a more traditional approach, focusing on reliability and experience. The best sales reps—and future leaders—can adjust their strategies to connect with every kind of customer.

The Golfer's Insight: How Alan Cooper Revolutionized Marketing

The Puzzling Path to Understanding Customers

Alan Cooper wasn't always the marketing legend he's known as today. In the late 1980s, he was a software developer buried in lines of code and consumed by the intricacies of technology. But something gnawed at him—no matter how sophisticated his programs were, they often missed the mark with users. The disconnect between the developers and the people using the software was glaring.

One day, while working on a new project, Alan stepped away from his desk to clear his mind. He found himself on a golf course, sharing a casual game with a client. As they strolled the green, their conversation drifted from casual banter to the challenges the client faced at work.

Cooper asked questions—not about code, but about the client's daily routines, frustrations, and aspirations. By the time the round was over, Cooper had gained an insight that struck him like lightning.

This wasn't just small talk. This was the key to bridging the gap he had been wrestling with for years.

The Clash Between Data and Humanity

Back in the office, Alan couldn't shake the memory of that golf course conversation. He began to see his clients as more than just roles or job titles. They were people with goals, pain points, and emotions that shaped their decisions.

The problem was most companies didn't think that way. Developers wrote software for faceless masses and marketers built campaigns for demographics, not people. Companies obsessed over numbers and generalizations, crafting products for "40–50-year-old men" or "millennial women," ignoring the individuality of their audience. The disconnect was staggering—and costly.

Alan knew there had to be a better way. Inspired by his golf course epiphany, he decided to create a fictional representation of his ideal client, rooted in the real-world insights he had gained. He gave this persona a name (Kathy), a backstory, and specific challenges. The software wasn't for "a user" anymore—it was for Kathy.

His colleagues were skeptical. Wasn't this too simplistic? But as Alan began applying personas to his projects, the results spoke for themselves. Clients raved about the usability and relevance of his designs. Slowly, his peers began to see the power of stepping into their customers' shoes.

The Birth of Buyer Personas

Alan didn't stop there. He evangelized the practice, showing teams how to create detailed, empathetic profiles of their ideal customers. These weren't mere avatars but rooted in research and real conversations. Alan bridged the gap between businesses and the people they served by giving a face to the faceless.

Years later, Alan Cooper became widely recognized as the originator of buyer personas, a concept that transformed software design, marketing, and sales. His insights taught companies to look beyond data points and see the human stories behind the numbers.

Today, his legacy lives on in boardrooms, creative sessions, and strategy meetings across industries. And it all started on a golf course, where Alan realized that understanding one customer's story could change how we connect with them all.

Key Takeaway: See the Bigger Picture

Insight isn't just a tool—it's a mindset. When you learn to see the world through your customer's eyes, you'll do more than close deals; you'll build trust, solve problems, and position yourself as a leader. Start now, and you'll discover that the skills you develop as a sales rep can carry you all the way to the top.

Action Exercises

1. **Develop Personas:** Write a one-page persona for one of your top customers, including their goals, challenges, and decision-making process. Use this to guide your next sales call.

2. **Map the Journey:** For a current prospect, outline their buyer's journey. Identify where they are in the process and adjust your strategy to meet them where they are.

3. **Practice Adaptability:** Choose two customers from different generations. Analyze their buying behaviors and preferences—then, experiment with tailoring your approach to each one.

17

The Sales Rep's Secret Weapon: Content Marketing

What if you could stand out in your industry—not because of flashy sales tactics, but because you genuinely help your customers? Content marketing isn't just a tool for big companies with marketing teams—it's the secret weapon for sales reps who want to build trust, grow their personal brand, and create lasting success. In this chapter, you'll learn how content marketing can transform your sales approach and set the foundation for your climb to the CEO's office.

The Tale of Ed and Larry: A Sales Rep's Guide to Trust

Larry's Wayward Calls

Larry was the friend everyone knew, but few wanted to hear from. His calls were predictable—always starting with feigned warmth and ending with a sales pitch.

"Hey, how's the family?" he'd ask. "Still coaching Billy's hockey team?"

Before you could answer, he'd dive into his latest product: vitamins, raffle tickets, or some network marketing scheme. Conversations with Larry weren't about catching up; they were a transaction waiting to happen.

You didn't block his number out of politeness, but you hesitated every time it flashed on your phone. You knew what was coming. Larry didn't reach out to give; he reached out to take.

Ed's Quiet Impact

Ed was different. He never called to sell, but his actions sold something far more important: trust. When you were stuck at work and your kids needed a ride to practice, Ed showed up. If you mentioned your plans to repaint your house, he'd share a list of reliable contractors he trusted, expecting nothing in return.

Ed wasn't just a friend; he was a resource. So, when Ed did have something to sell— something he genuinely believed would help—you didn't hesitate to listen. You knew his pitch came from a place of honesty, not opportunism. And often, you'd buy; not just because you trusted the product, but because you trusted Ed.

Ed didn't need to push or persuade. His consistent service built a bridge of goodwill that Larry could only dream of crossing.

Be like Ed, Not Larry

Content marketing is about being the Ed of your field. It's about building relationships, providing value, and earning trust long before you make an ask.

Larry's approach—showing up only to take—is old-school, transactional, and doomed to fail. Customers have caller IDs for people like Larry; they also have spam filters. But Ed? Ed has their attention because he earned it through consistency and care.

The same principle applies in business. When you offer value freely, solve problems without strings, and engage authentically, you build a reputation that makes customers want to hear from you. And when the time comes to pitch your product or service, they'll listen— because you're not just another Larry.

Moral of the Story: Be an Ed

To move from sales rep to CEO, you must think like Ed. Build trust. Provide value. Engage your customers with honesty. Your audience isn't just looking for solutions; they're looking for someone they can believe in.

Larry might sell a few raffle tickets. But Ed? Ed builds a legacy.

Why Every Sales Rep Needs to Master Content Marketing

Imagine walking into a meeting where the customer already knows your name, values your expertise, and trusts your advice. That's the power of content marketing. It flips the traditional sales process on its head. Instead of chasing prospects, they come to you.

Content marketing isn't about selling. It's about teaching. It's about consistently showing up with information that helps your audience solve problems. As a sales rep, your job is understanding your customers better than anyone else. Use that knowledge to create content they actually care about— answers to their most challenging questions, tips for improving their workflow, or insights about the future of their industry.

Think about it. When you consistently share valuable content, your customers see you as more than a salesperson. You become their go-to person for advice. That kind of trust isn't built overnight, but once it's there, it's unshakable. And trust leads to sales. Not just one-off deals, but partnerships that last.

Content marketing also future-proofs your career. Sales can be a tough game. When markets shift or products lose their edge, your ability to create value through your personal brand will set you apart. That's how you get noticed by leadership. That's how you move from being a sales rep to being a leader.

You don't need to be a professional writer or marketer to get started. Begin with what you know: Answer common questions. Share stories of challenges and solutions. Post a quick tip on LinkedIn or record a short video for your audience. Authenticity matters more than polish. People respond to real, relatable voices.

The key is consistency. Content marketing isn't a one-and-done effort. It's a habit. It's about showing up, week after week, with something that adds value. Over time, you'll build a body of work that doesn't just drive sales—it creates a reputation. And that reputation will be the foundation of your journey from the sales floor to the boardroom.

The Turning Point: When Sales Met Strategy

The Crossroads of Change

In 2011, LASIK surgery was undergoing a seismic shift. The method surgeons had relied on for years was being replaced by a newer, more advanced—and more expensive—approach. At Sightpath Medical, we faced a difficult decision: Stick with the older, familiar method and watch profits dwindle, or make a bold leap to embrace the new technology.

The stakes were high. Transitioning would mean upsetting our sales team, who relied on the older service to meet their numbers. Tensions began to brew. The team saw the change as a threat, not an opportunity. How could we convince them—and our market—that this was the right move?

A Lesson from Netflix

The pressure to justify our decision mounted. I had just started a blog called Connected Rep and wanted to know if it could be more than a personal project. Could I use it to rally our team and customers around this pivotal change?

Then, inspiration struck from an unlikely source: Netflix. Around the same time, Netflix announced it was discontinuing its DVD mail-in service to go all-in on streaming. The backlash was swift. Critics hammered the decision, and customers were furious. But CEO Reed Hastings didn't waver. He saw where the future was heading and stayed the course, even as the company's stock took a beating.

That story resonated deeply with me. Like Netflix, we were phasing out an outdated service that no longer aligned with our vision. But understanding the need for change wasn't enough—we had to bring others along on the journey.

I wrote a blog post titled "Stop the Beating of Netflix," drawing parallels between Netflix's decision and ours. I argued that sometimes, to grow, you must endure the pain of transformation. I explained how Sightpath's move wasn't just necessary—it was a step toward a stronger, more profitable future.

The Power of Persuasion

Armed with my blog post, I took the message directly to the market. I shared it on LinkedIn, giving our sales team a straightforward customer narrative. But that wasn't enough. I needed to walk the talk.

I joined one of our sales reps on a field visit. We met with surgeons face-to-face. As I explained our decision, the reasons became tangible for them and for the rep by my side. He saw how framing the change as a vision for the future shifted the conversation from resistance to acceptance.

The results were striking. The sales team began using the blog and LinkedIn posts as tools to answer tough questions. They started seeing the transition as a chance to lead, not a burden to bear. By connecting a broader market story to our own, we found a way to navigate the turbulence and emerge stronger.

The Takeaway

Change is rarely easy, especially when it disrupts established habits. But with a clear message and a willingness to engage directly, you can turn resistance into momentum. For a sales rep on the path to becoming a CEO, this story serves as a reminder that sometimes leadership means making tough decisions and finding the right way to tell the story behind them.

Key Takeaway: Take the Long View and Plant Seeds Today for Tomorrow's Harvest

Content marketing isn't just about generating leads; it's about creating connections. It helps you stand out in a world full of noise by offering something most sales reps overlook— genuine value. When you consistently provide helpful insights, your audience will remember you when it's time to buy. And the best part? The relationships you build today will continue to pay dividends throughout your career. Start small, stay consistent, and watch your influence grow.

Action Exercises

1. **Find Your Niche:** Identify one area where you have unique expertise or insights. Write down three common questions customers ask in that area and outline short answers you could turn into content.

2. **Create Your First Post:** Pick a question from your list and create a simple LinkedIn post answering it. Keep it short, conversational, and useful. Publish it and invite feedback from your audience.

3. **Build a Content Calendar:** Plan to create and share one piece of content each week for the next month. Use your customers' biggest challenges as inspiration and track which topics get the best response.

PART SIX

Understanding the Attributes of a Leader

Our journey from sales rep to CEO began with a vision—you have to want this success and be clear about the steps you will take and the strategies you will use to achieve it. From that starting point, the rest of the journey has led us outward from your own internal mindset, through your organization and its various functions, and out into the world in which you operate, a world made up of metrics and customers who must be understood.

Now, in the final part of this book, it's time to bring the journey right back to you as we focus on the attributes of a leader that you will need to understand and develop if you are to finally assume the office of CEO. Some of those attributes are perhaps obvious, like the ability to communicate well and build trust. Others are less discussed, like the ability to listen and admit mistakes.

All are essential attributes on the road from sales rep to CEO. The final attribute is maybe the most surprising and important of all. As we shall see, if you want to exalt yourself and reach high office, the best way to get there is on the humble road of humility.

18

The True Cost of Hidden Truths: The Importance of Radical Transparency

In the high-pressure world of sales, the temptation to cut corners can be overwhelming. But when you trade integrity for short-term gains, you set yourself—and your career—on shaky ground. This chapter uncovers how transparency can transform your work, build trust, and solidify your path to leadership.

The Price of Radical Transparency

The Promise of a New Tool

Throughout my career, I have prided myself on transparency—a principle I carried into every sales presentation board meeting and decision. Honesty was my anchor, even when the waters got rough. One year, a junior financial analyst introduced a new budgeting model. It looked sleek, sophisticated, and promising—precisely the kind of innovation a growing company craves.

The model churned out numbers that painted an exciting picture of our future. It became the foundation of the following year's budget, which the board of directors enthusiastically approved. But sometimes, even the brightest tools hide a flaw that changes everything.

An Uncomfortable Truth

Weeks later, as we dug deeper into the numbers, my team uncovered a critical error in the model. Its flaw? It overstated depreciation, inflating our earnings before interest, taxes, depreciation, and amortization (EBITDA) projections. The implications were serious—our approved budget hinged on unrealistic expectations, and the board was already holding us to this inflated standard.

I had two choices. I could stay silent and hope to manage the gap as the year unfolded, knowing that failure to hit targets would cast doubt on my leadership and result in reduced annual bonuses for employees. Or I could expose the error, risking my credibility and, more alarmingly, embarrassing a trusted analyst.

I chose transparency.

With the weight of the truth on my shoulders, I went directly to the board and laid out the error with as much clarity and professionalism as I could muster. My words were met with silence, then questions, then frustration. The analyst, whose model had failed us, felt terrible. Even though I took responsibility for what happened, the person left the company soon after.

My decision came at a cost. While the mistake wasn't mine, my insistence on exposing it created tension.

The Quiet Victory

In the aftermath, I reflected on what I'd done. Transparency had cost me politically, but it secured a stronger foundation for the company's operations. The budget was corrected, and the company moved forward on realistic terms.

I reaffirmed my belief that leadership isn't about avoiding conflict—it's about making choices that align with your values, even when inconvenient. Transparency may not always win you favor, but it ensures you can face yourself—and your team—with integrity intact.

Sometimes, the most challenging path is the only path forward. And as I have learned time and again, it sets the stage for authentic leadership.

Why Transparency Builds Leaders

Transparency: Your Most Valuable Asset

Success in sales often feels like a numbers game, but numbers without integrity are meaningless. Transparency is not just a virtue—it's a strategic advantage. It builds trust, enables better decisions, and creates opportunities for long-term growth.

Trust Is Currency

Customers buy from people they trust. You build credibility when you're honest about what your product can or cannot do. A straightforward "We can't meet that timeline, but here's how we can help" often wins more loyalty than an overpromise that leads to disappointment.

Trust earned through transparency is hard to break—and even harder for competitors to replicate.

Clarity Drives Results

In sales, clear communication is the backbone of solid relationships. Transparency ensures that your customers and internal teams know what to expect. When you report a situation honestly to your manager—whether it's a delay, a missed quota, or a deal on shaky ground—it positions you as a reliable partner, not just a performer.

A Reputation You Can Stand On

Word travels fast in business. Reps who cut corners gain a reputation that sticks—and not in a good way. Conversely, transparency solidifies your brand as a professional who values integrity over short-term wins.

Examples to Emulate

Look at leaders like Howard Root, the ex-CEO of Cardiovascular Systems, who fought a five-year federal prosecution over off-label marketing, detailing the ordeal in his book *Cardiac Arrest*. Root's refusal to bend the truth under pressure sets an example of resilience and moral clarity. Sales reps who aim to lead must follow suit, showing that transparency isn't just about avoiding trouble—it's about actively building a foundation for trust and respect.

The Truth Is Heavy but Strong

The office was quiet that morning. I held the paper in my hand, though I didn't need it. I knew the numbers by heart. They were bad. Worse than bad—they meant the project wouldn't work as planned. The customer had trusted me, and now I had to face them with the truth.

I took a deep breath and called Jim. He was the VP at a mid-sized hospital group, and he had bet a lot on this deal. We'd promised his team an instrument system to save time and reduce costs. On paper, everything had checked out. In practice, we'd miscalculated. I told him we needed to talk, face to face, so I'd fly out to see him.

The meeting was scheduled for two days later, and the room felt smaller than I remembered. Jim arrived right on time, his usual calm confidence masking the stress I knew he was under. I didn't waste time.

"Jim," I said, "we've rerun the numbers, and the instrument replacement model won't deliver what we projected. The savings won't materialize the way we'd promised."

His face didn't change at first, but I saw the tension in his jaw. I didn't try to soften it. Instead, I explained how we'd gone wrong, why it happened, and what steps we were already taking to fix it. I offered him a clear exit if he wanted to back out or a revised plan if he was willing to give us time.

He stared at me for a long moment, then leaned back in his chair. "You could've covered this up," he said. "Passed the blame or spun the numbers."

"I know," I replied. "But that wouldn't have helped either of us in the long run."

To my surprise, he nodded. "I respect that. Let's figure out how to fix this."

The conversation that followed wasn't easy, but it was honest. We revised the scope, adjusted expectations, and came up with a plan that worked. The system didn't roll out on schedule, but when it did, it met the revised goals. More importantly, it strengthened my relationship with Jim.

A year later, Jim called me for another project. "I knew I could trust you," he said.

The truth is heavy, but it holds things together. That day it proved I was someone worth betting on.

Key Takeaway: Make Honesty Your Leadership Brand

Transparency is more than an ethical stance—it's your competitive edge. It shows customers, colleagues, and executives that you value trust and results over shortcuts. The habits of honesty you build today will shape the leader you become tomorrow. Start by owning your truth and watch how others rally behind you.

Action Exercises

1. **Review Your Pipeline Honestly:** Audit your current deals. Identify any that are overpromised or unrealistic and communicate updates to your manager.

2. **Have Trust-Building Conversations:** Reach out to one customer this week to give an update—good or bad. Use the conversation to reinforce their trust in you as a partner.

3. **Own a Mistake Publicly:** Identify a past misstep that impacted a deal or relationship. Discuss what you've learned and how you've corrected it with your team or manager.

19

Where the Buck Stops: Owning Accountability

The numbers don't lie, but people often try to make them tell a different story. As a sales rep with aspirations for the corner office, you need to master the art of honest financial discussions. This chapter shows why owning the numbers—good, bad, or ugly—builds trust, credibility, and leadership.

The Fork in the Road: A Lesson in Accountability and Leadership

A Fresh Deal and a Fresh Start

The ink on the acquisition papers was barely dry, and the team was eager to prove that the move was a success. We had acquired a small but promising company built by a single operator—someone who knew every corner of his business but was now stepping into a new role as a sales rep.

The former owner had transitioned well—or so it seemed. He brought a blend of field experience and deep customer relationships that gave us confidence he'd excel as part of our team. For me, as the CEO, this acquisition was more than a transaction. It was a litmus test of our strategy, instincts, and ability to integrate a business while maintaining customer trust.

Four months in, the integration seemed on track. Sales were steady, customers appeared happy, and we were optimistic. Until the day our new sales rep walked into my office.

"We Have a Problem"

The look on his face told me the news wasn't good before he said a word. He sat down and leaned forward as if to lighten the weight of his message by sharing it quickly.

"I have to let you know that we have a problem with two large accounts," he said, his voice steady but measured.

He didn't have to spell out the stakes. These weren't just any accounts; they were cornerstone clients from his book of business—clients whose loyalty had helped justify the purchase price we'd paid. Losing them wouldn't just sting; it would call the entire deal into question. For him, the consequences in his new role were minimal. But the failure would cast long shadows for me and the rest of the leadership team who had championed this acquisition.

I asked for details, and he laid it out plainly. The problems weren't small. Pricing disputes, customer dissatisfaction, and a sense that their long-time loyalty wasn't reciprocated. It was the kind of slow erosion that could snowball into outright defection.

I could feel the heat of frustration rising, but I held it back. This was a moment to lead, not to blame.

"Can we save them?" I asked.

He didn't hesitate. "I think we can. But it'll take work."

Earning Trust, Brick by Brick

And work we did. We spent weeks rebuilding what had been strained. Together, we visited those accounts. We sat down with their leadership teams to not argue but listen. It was uncomfortable at first. I remember one of their VPs leaning back in his chair, arms crossed as if daring us to explain why they shouldn't take their business elsewhere.

The former owner stepped up. He spoke with authenticity and humility, acknowledging the missteps but also reminding them of the long-standing relationship they had shared. I followed his lead, promising—and delivering—a faster, more reliable service process.

Slowly, the ice thawed. By the time we left, we had resecured their commitment. It wasn't just a win for those accounts; it was a lesson for me about what it means to be accountable. The former owner didn't have to care—he could've shrugged it off and left the mess for us to clean up. But he didn't. He showed up.

The Fork in the Road

In moments like these, leadership isn't about titles or roles. It's about choosing the harder path when it's easier to walk away. That day, I saw the kind of accountability that separates those who coast from those who lead.

As a sales rep, you'll have your forks in the road. The easy path might seem tempting, but the road to becoming a CEO is paved with hard choices and the courage to own the outcome.

Reporting the Tough Truths

Why It's Better to Face the Music

Every sales rep will encounter bad numbers. A dropped deal. A dwindling account. A forecast that misses the mark. These moments test your mettle because they're uncomfortable, even painful, to share. Yet, the decision to hide or delay these truths is where careers start to unravel. Transparency might sting in the short term, but it builds the foundation for trust—and trust is what fuels long-term success.

Imagine you are seeing signs of disengagement with your loyal customer. Instead of sharing your concerns with your manager, you hesitate. You hope things will improve. Weeks pass. The account slips away. Now, instead of being seen as a proactive problem solver, you're the rep who let a key client walk without raising an alarm. That's the cost of silence.

Transparency transforms these moments of crisis into opportunities for growth. Early warnings give your team time to act, adjust, and potentially recover the account. They also show that you're accountable, perceptive, and invested in the company's success. These traits separate good reps from great ones—and great reps from future CEOs.

Breaking the Cycle of Avoidance

Avoiding tough financial conversations is tempting because it feels protective. But it does the opposite. When you sugarcoat forecasts or underreport risks, you set up a fall. The truth always surfaces, and the delay erodes your credibility. Credibility, once lost, is nearly impossible to regain.

Think of transparency as a currency. It buys goodwill with leadership, colleagues, and customers. Managers don't expect perfection, but they do expect honesty. You're more likely to get support if you approach them early with potential problems. And when customers feel like partners rather than targets, they're more likely to stay loyal—even in tough times.

Lessons from Leadership

Transparency is more than a career skill; it's a leadership trait. CEOs don't have the luxury of hiding the truth. Their success depends on owning the numbers and leading through them. As a sales rep, practicing this now signals to others that you're capable of bigger responsibilities. It shows you value the company's long-term success over your immediate comfort.

The Price of Dishonesty: How Sarah Lost the Big Deal

Building Trust on Shaky Ground

Sarah was a star sales rep, the kind everyone envied. Her name was whispered in admiration at company meetings, and she was on the brink of her biggest win yet—a deal with a major hospital system that would crown her as the top rep in the company. For nearly a year, she poured her energy into this opportunity, meeting surgeons, administrators, and finance teams, selling her surgical devices as the ultimate solution for better patient outcomes.

The hospital was intrigued but cautious. The CFO asked for a comprehensive cost breakdown, wanting to account for upfront costs, future fees, and maintenance expenses. Sarah's pitch was polished, her smile unwavering. She promised value, innovation, and long-term savings. But in the back of her mind, she knew the hidden costs lurking beneath the surface— annual maintenance fees that escalated and pricey updates required for the devices to stay functional. Sarah hesitated. She needed this deal to cement her reputation. Surely, they wouldn't notice. Surely, they'd understand once the papers were signed.

Cracks in the Façade

The CFO wasn't buying charm alone. His meticulous and wary team kept pressing Sarah for the full picture. Sarah wavered, offering a partial breakdown that danced around the uncomfortable details. She left out the escalating maintenance fees and expensive replacement parts, banking on the hospital's urgency to finalize the deal.

But the CFO's team grew suspicious. Numbers weren't adding up. They bypassed Sarah and went directly to her company's finance department. There, the truth spilled out: A stark picture of hidden costs that Sarah had deliberately obscured. Maintenance fees that climbed year by year.

Replacement parts that bled budgets dry. Updates with price tags the size of a small car.

The CFO was livid. Trust had been shattered, and trust was everything. The hospital immediately killed the deal, pivoting to a competitor who had been honest. Sarah's carefully built year of work crumbled in an instant.

The Weight of Truth

The fallout was swift and brutal. Sarah's boss summoned her for a meeting that could have been scripted by disaster itself. Still reeling from the hospital's scathing feedback, the executive team demanded answers. "Why didn't you disclose the costs?" they asked, their disappointment heavier than their words. Sarah had no good reply.

Her reputation unraveled. Clients who once sang her praises grew wary, questioning her transparency. Leads dried up. She was placed on a performance improvement plan, her career suddenly hanging by a thread.

For the hospital, the betrayal served as a warning beacon. But for Sarah, it became a painful, lasting lesson: Honesty isn't optional in sales—it's the cornerstone of credibility. If she'd been upfront about the costs, the hospital might have found a way to make it work. By choosing deception, she lost the deal and her standing as a trusted partner in the industry.

In the sales world, a reputation for honesty is worth more than a single deal. Sarah's story echoes an age-old truth: Trust, once broken, is nearly impossible to rebuild. This story is a stark reminder for those aspiring to climb the ladder from sales rep to CEO—never let short-term wins compromise your long-term integrity.

Key Takeaway: Hard Truths Build Real Leaders

Transparency is not about avoiding problems—it's about confronting them with integrity. When you own the numbers and communicate openly, you show that you value trust over temporary appearances. The path to leadership is paved with difficult conversations, and every one of them strengthens your character. Take them head-on, and you'll find that clarity breeds respect—and respect fuels success.

Action Exercises

1. **Proactively Report a Risk:** Review your accounts for any signs of trouble. Identify one potential risk and report it to your manager before it becomes a problem. Be prepared with clear facts and a proposed solution.

2. **Track Honesty's Impact:** In your next meeting with leadership, share a financial update with complete transparency. Note how this builds trust or fosters collaboration. Reflect on how honesty affects your reputation and relationships.

3. **Have an Open Conversation with a Customer:** Choose one customer and honestly share a financial challenge or upcoming change. Focus on fostering trust and problem-solving together. Observe how they respond and how the discussion impacts your partnership.

20

Fragile but Strong: How to Build Trust That Lasts

Trust is a fragile thing, but it can be your greatest strength. As a sales rep, every deal you close and every relationship you nurture hinges on it. Trust begins and ends with transparency. This chapter unpacks how being open—both inside your company and with your customers— builds the credibility and loyalty you need to thrive as a sales professional and a future CEO.

The Deal That Changed the Game

The Secret Deals

For years, the sales team at Sightpath Medical believed secrecy was their best weapon.

They thought they could work on deals quietly, outmaneuvering Alcon, the market leader and Sightpath's key supplier. Each time, the plan backfired. Somehow, Alcon's field sales team always caught wind of the deals, igniting competitive skirmishes.

These clashes didn't just strain relationships—they left both companies worse off, with deals either falling apart or yielding subpar results. It was a toxic cycle fueled by mistrust, and it had gone on far too long.

A House Divided

When I took over as head of sales, I inherited a mess. The sales teams on both sides were stuck in a zero-sum mindset. Each deal became a battlefield, with Sightpath and Alcon fighting for scraps instead of collaborating for success. The mistrust was palpable. But I knew that if we didn't fix this dynamic, it would only hurt our ability to grow and jeopardize the future of our partnership with Alcon.

That's when I reached out to Bill Doran, the VP of sales at Alcon. Bill and I sat down for an honest conversation. We didn't sugarcoat the situation. We admitted the mutual failures, acknowledged the friction, and recognized the opportunity we were squandering by working against each other. It wasn't an easy conversation, but it was a necessary one.

Building the Bridge

Together, Bill and I decided to change the game. We created a culture of communication and transparency between our teams. No more secret deals. No more blindsiding. Instead, we aligned our efforts, openly sharing goals and strategies to work together as true partners.

Over time, Alcon transformed from a rival into a channel sales partner. The shift didn't happen overnight, but as trust grew, so did the results. Deals closed faster, customer satisfaction improved, and both companies reaped the rewards of collaboration. What once felt like an impossible divide became a powerful partnership that propelled both teams forward.

The lesson was clear: Trust and transparency are not just ideals—they're the foundation for winning together. I carried this principle with me on my journey from sales rep to CEO.

Transparency: The Hidden Superpower

Transparency isn't flashy, but it's powerful. It separates the opportunists from the long-haulers. As a sales rep, you might think your job is to make the sale, hit the target, and move on. But transparency is your hidden superpower if you want more than short-term wins.

Think of your work as building bridges. One side is your company, and the other is your customer. The bridge itself is trust. If you compromise on transparency, you weaken the structure. Maybe you withhold lousy news about a delay, thinking it's harmless, or inflate projections to satisfy leadership. These cracks might hold for a while, but sooner or later, they'll collapse. And when they do, you're not just losing deals—you're losing credibility.

Transparency isn't about airing every detail. It's about being honest when it matters. Internally, this might mean owning up to challenges and asking for help. For example, a sales rep who admits they're struggling to close a deal opens the door to support—whether that's strategic advice from the leadership team or insights from marketing. Concealing struggles, on the other hand, isolates you. And in sales, isolation is a dangerous place to be.

Externally, transparency builds trust with customers. Imagine you're working with a long-time client. A new competitor has entered the market with a cheaper and flashier product. You know your company's offering is superior in the long run but lacks the bells and whistles. A less transparent rep might dismiss the competitor outright or avoid the conversation altogether. However, a transparent rep acknowledges the competition before focusing on the enduring value their own company provides. This approach not only keeps the client—it strengthens the relationship. Why?

Because they trust you to tell them the truth.

Transparency isn't a one-time effort; it's a culture you cultivate. Start small. If you're worried about missing your monthly number, share this with your manager—not as an excuse, but as an opportunity to collaborate. If a customer asks about a potential delay, don't sugarcoat it. Explain the challenge and what you're doing to fix it. These moments of honesty may feel uncomfortable, but they're investments in your reputation. Over time, they pay dividends.

And when you begin to think beyond the sales rep role, transparency becomes even more critical. CEOs don't succeed on numbers alone; they succeed because people believe in them. Transparency is what makes people believe in you—not because you're perfect, but because you're real.

Navigating the Storm: How Transparency Saved the Business

The Storm on the Horizon

In February 2013, Sightpath Medical faced a storm it never saw coming. The Department of Justice launched an investigation into alleged kickback activity with its physician customers. Rumors swirled. Questions arose. For years, the dark cloud lingered, threatening to overshadow everything Sightpath had worked to build.

By August 2017, the weight of the prospect of upcoming litigation had become too much. The company decided to settle the case, not because of guilt but to avoid the endless distraction and expense of legal battles. Part of the settlement required Sightpath to enter into a five-year corporate integrity agreement (CIA). While the settlement admitted no wrongdoing, the media latched onto the story. Headlines weren't kind, and trust became a fragile commodity. For a company built on relationships, this wasn't just a legal issue—it was existential.

Walking the Tightrope

The question wasn't just how Sightpath would survive the bad press but how the company could maintain trust without fanning the flames. Internally, leadership had to walk a tightrope. Should we address the situation head-on or let silence speak for us?

The strategy was clear: transparency when asked but silence otherwise. Sightpath decided to "starve the story" externally. No press conferences. No grand defenses. Instead, we focused on communicating and equipping the team to navigate the inevitable conversations with some customers.

This approach was not without challenges. A critical part of the settlement required compliance language to be added to all service agreements. For the sales team, this new language was a minefield. Customers wanted explanations. Sales reps needed guidance. Leadership quickly realized the importance of transparency—not just with customers but within their own ranks.

Meetings were held. Scripts were written. Reps were trained to handle difficult conversations with honesty and tact. The company leaned on its long history of service and integrity to reassure nervous clients. Yet, doubt remained: Would it be enough?

Resolution: The Light at the End

It worked. Of more than 800 customers, only one chose to leave. That single loss was a testament to the trust Sightpath had built over the years. Customers valued the transparency, the willingness to answer tough questions, and the absence of defensive posturing.

By focusing on open communication when it mattered, Sightpath preserved its reputation and strengthened its relationships. The company emerged from the storm with battle scars and a renewed understanding of the power of honesty in leadership.

The lesson for a sales rep aspiring to become a CEO is clear: When trust is on the line, silence can be dangerous. Equip your team, face the questions, and let transparency be your compass. It might just save your business.

Key Takeaway: How Transparency Elevates Your Career

Transparency isn't just a tool; it's a mindset. It's what keeps your bridge intact as you navigate the challenges of sales and leadership. Trust isn't built overnight, but it's destroyed in a heartbeat. By choosing transparency, you ensure your foundation is unshakable. Being transparent takes courage, but it's worth it. It's how you gain the respect of your team, the loyalty of your customers, and the belief of your leadership. These aren't just traits of a great sales rep—they're the traits of a future CEO.

Action Exercises

1. **Internal Transparency:** Reflect on a recent time when you hesitated to share a challenge with your manager or team. Write down what you could have said instead and plan to discuss it openly.

2. **Customer Transparency:** Identify a client relationship where you've avoided addressing a difficult topic. Practice framing the conversation honestly and positively.

3. **Trust Audit:** List three ways you've earned trust through transparency this month. What worked, and how can you build on it?

21

Admitting Mistakes: Why It's Right to Say "I Was Wrong"

Mistakes are inevitable in sales and leadership. How you handle them defines your reputation, shapes your relationships, and builds—or breaks—trust. In this chapter, you'll learn why admitting you're wrong isn't a weakness but a strength and how mastering this skill can set you apart as a leader on your journey from sales rep to CEO.

Owning My Mistake: A Parking Lot Lesson in Leadership

The Cost of Overstepping

Dr. Art Mruchuck was an ophthalmologist in Medina, New York, and, as you might remember from Chapter twelve, my first encounter with him was a masterclass in missteps. I'd shown up at his hospital unannounced to discuss a delinquent invoice, only to be promptly thrown out by the materials manager. When I later called Dr. Mruchuck to smooth things over, his words cut deep: "You need to act like a professional. Don't ever visit me again without scheduling an appointment."

I was humiliated—and angry. But as the sting faded, I realized something uncomfortable: He was right. I'd been wrong to assume my urgency gave me the right to disregard another person's time and processes. The more I thought about it, the more I knew I had to make amends

—not just for the relationship but for myself.

The Power of an Apology

Several weeks later, I found myself waiting in the doctor's parking lot, nerves gnawing as I watched for Dr. Mruchuck. It wasn't a strategic move—it was personal. I needed to face him directly and own my mistake.

When he finally emerged after surgery, I approached him cautiously. "Dr. Mruchuck," I said, my voice steady despite my racing heart. "I apologize for being unannounced again, but I wanted to tell you something important. I was wrong the other day. I overstepped, and I ask for your forgiveness."

For a moment, his face was unreadable. The silence felt heavier than I could bear. Then, his expression softened. "I give you points for persistence, young man," he said. "I accept your apology. Now, next time, do it the right way—call my office and schedule an appointment." Relief swept over me, but his words carried a deeper lesson. Owning up to a mistake wasn't just the right thing to do—it was an act of strength.

Building Trust Through Humility

I didn't squander my second chance. Over the next several months, I called ahead, scheduled visits, and ensured I respected the doctor's time. As I did so, our relationship grew stronger. Dr. Mruchuck became more than just a customer; he became a mentor. He taught me about ophthalmology, but more importantly, he showed me the value of trust, humility, and accountability.

Looking back, I realize the turning point wasn't just about persistence. It was about admitting I was wrong and taking action to correct it. That parking lot conversation wasn't a setback—it was a step forward in becoming the kind of professional and person I aspired to be.

The Lesson

In sales and life, mistakes are inevitable. What defines us is how we respond. Admitting I was wrong didn't make me weaker; it made me stronger. It opened doors to trust, respect, and growth—lessons that have stayed with me and played a key part on my journey from sales rep to CEO. Dr. Mruchuck's forgiveness was a gift, but the real transformation came from owning my misstep and striving to do better.

The Courage to Admit You're Wrong

Admitting you're wrong feels uncomfortable. It exposes vulnerabilities, challenges your pride, and risks your reputation—at least, that's what it seems like. But admitting mistakes is a display of courage, accountability, and self-awareness. It's what separates average performers from exceptional leaders.

Sales reps face a unique pressure to be flawless. Every client interaction feels like a tightrope walk where even small errors can jeopardize a deal. However, customers value honesty more than perfection. When you admit a mistake, you show them you're human and, more importantly, that you respect the relationship. That respect often outweighs any disappointment caused by the error itself.

Take this scenario: You misquote a pricing structure. Instead of dodging the issue or blaming a colleague, you own up to it. "I gave you incorrect information earlier, and I want to correct that now." This moment of honesty might feel like handing your client a reason to walk away, but it often has the opposite effect. It builds credibility, showing that you prioritize the partnership over the sale.

For aspiring CEOs, the stakes are even higher. Leaders who admit mistakes create a culture where transparency thrives. Team members feel safe taking calculated risks and innovating without fear of blame. By modeling this behavior as a sales rep, you lay the foundation for a leadership style that inspires trust and loyalty.

Owning your mistakes also sharpens your problem-solving skills. When you're not distracted by denial or excuses, you can focus on understanding what went wrong and how to fix it. This proactive approach not only resolves the immediate issue but also prevents similar problems down the road.

Admitting mistakes isn't about groveling or diminishing your authority. It's about showing that you value progress over pride. As you demonstrate this to your clients, colleagues, and superiors, you'll notice something powerful: They start to see you as a leader who can guide with authenticity and strength, as the following story shows.

The Cost of Truth

The Late Call

It was a quiet Thursday afternoon when the phone rang. One of my best sales reps, Tom, was on the line. Tom wasn't just any rep; he was sharp, ambitious, and always knew how to close a deal. But there was a crack in his usual confidence today. His voice was uneven, like a man walking a tightrope without a net.

"I've got to talk to you about something," he said, his words weighed down. "It's about The Center for Specialty Surgery."

The Center was no ordinary account. It was a flagship client for us, a key that opened doors to a larger network of surgical centers. Securing their business had been a high point for the team, a win that validated months of effort. But now, Tom sounded like a man standing in the shadow of a wreck. My mind raced through possibilities. Had we overpromised? Was the client unhappy?

"I made a mistake," he finally admitted. The words came slow and deliberate like he was unloading bricks one by one.

The Domino Effect

Tom confessed that during the pitch to The Center, he'd quoted a discount structure without checking with pricing first. It wasn't intentional, but he'd let his enthusiasm outrun his discipline in his zeal to close the deal. Now, The Center's leadership was holding us to that number—a number that would cut into our margins more than anyone had anticipated.

"I thought I could manage it," Tom said. "I thought I could fix it before it became a problem, but it's too late now."

In that moment, I didn't know what was worse—his mistake or the fact that he'd been sitting on it for weeks, trying to cover his tracks. Anger stirred in me. This wasn't the kind of thing you could sweep under the rug. Our entire profit and loss for the quarter could be affected, and worse, it might erode the trust we'd built with The Center if we renegotiated.

But as I listened to Tom, something shifted. His voice cracked with sincerity. He wasn't making excuses. He owned it, fully and completely.

"I should've come to you right away," he said. "I screwed up, and I'll do whatever it takes to make it right."

There it was—the kind of accountability you don't teach. You either have it, or you don't.

The Second Chance

We worked late into the night, brainstorming scenarios to salvage the situation. By morning, we had a plan. Tom called The Center for Specialty Surgery and explained the miscommunication. He took the hit straight and honestly, without blaming anyone else. Then, he pivoted, offering creative solutions that added value to The Center while protecting our bottom line.

It wasn't perfect, but it worked. The Center appreciated the honesty, and we preserved the account. More than that, Tom preserved something less tangible but more valuable—my respect.

Tom's honesty didn't just fix the problem; it transformed how I saw him. In his mistake, he showed me his character. He wasn't just a sales rep chasing numbers. He was someone who could shoulder the weight of responsibility and own the consequences of his actions. That's the kind of person who can grow into a leader.

When I think back on that day, it's not the mistake I remember most—it's the courage it took to admit it. Mistakes are inevitable in sales, business, and life. What defines you is what you do after. Tom proved that even a stumble can become a step forward if you face it with honesty and resolve.

When I finally sat in the CEO's chair, I carried that lesson like a talisman. Not every problem is about avoiding mistakes. Sometimes, it's about how you respond when the cracks show. That's where trust is forged, and that's where leaders are made.

Key Takeaway: Own It, Learn from It, Move Forward

Admitting mistakes isn't just a professional skill; it's a way of life for great leaders. It teaches humility, fosters trust, and clears the path for meaningful growth. Every error is an opportunity to prove that you prioritize the truth over your ego and the relationship over the sale.

Those are the traits of a leader others want to follow.

Action Exercises

1. **Write Your "Mistake Playbook":** Think back on three mistakes you've made in your career. For each, write what went wrong,

whether you admitted the error, and what you learned. Use this as a personal guide to handle future missteps.

2. **Practice Transparent Communication:** The next time you make an error, admit it within 24 hours. Notice how addressing it early impacts the situation and the responses of those involved.

3. **Observe Leadership in Action:** Watch how your manager or senior leaders handle their mistakes. What can you emulate? What would you do differently?

22

The Key to Turning Good to Great: Communication

Communication isn't just about words. It's about clarity, connection, and direction. For a sales rep aiming to lead, it's the skill that turns a good team into a great one. In this chapter, you'll learn how to use communication to align teams, foster collaboration, and build trust— traits essential for any future CEO.

The Price of Perspective

A CFO's Wake-Up Call

The numbers were hard to ignore. Month after month, Tony, the CFO, flagged the declining average selling price. It wasn't just a blip on the radar—it was a trend. To Tony, who lived and breathed margins and spreadsheets, it was a red flag.

At the next leadership meeting, Tony dropped the bombshell. "I'd like to discuss changing the sales compensation plan," he said, his tone firm. "Going forward, sales reps won't be paid on revenue alone. Their commissions will also be tied to profit."

Sitting across the table as head of sales, I could feel the temperature drop in the room. I knew my team's reaction before they even heard the news. They were already stretched thin, hustling to close deals in a fiercely competitive market. We'd never asked them to focus on profit margins—something beyond their control—and I knew it wouldn't go over well.

Tony's logic was sound from a financial perspective. Margins were shrinking, and the company needed to protect its bottom line. But I knew my team. I knew how hard they fought for every dollar in the field. This wasn't just a policy shift but a fundamental challenge to how they saw their role in the company.

The Clash Between Numbers and Reality

The backlash came quickly. The sales team was livid. "We can't control costs," one rep said in frustration during a call. "How are we supposed to be responsible for what it takes to make or deliver the product?" Another chimed in, "What's next? Negotiating labor rates with the operating room techs?"

I heard them out, knowing they weren't wrong. The team could influence pricing to some degree, but they couldn't control the costs of manufacturing, labor, or logistics. And while Tony's concerns about shrinking margins were valid, the new plan felt like an unfair burden on sales.

I wasn't just the head of sales; I was the bridge between my team and the executive leadership. If I didn't step in, the divide between finance and sales would only grow wider.

At our next leadership meeting, I addressed Tony directly. "I get where you're coming from," I said. "You're looking at the numbers; margins are critical to our survival. But from the sales team's perspective, tying commissions to profit feels like setting them up to fail. They don't control what it costs to produce or deliver our services."

Tony didn't back down. "If we don't focus on profit, Joel, there won't be a company left to sell anything," he said.

I nodded. "I hear you. But this can't be a one-sided solution. If we're going to ask the team to focus on profitability, we need to give them visibility into the costs and a way to influence the outcomes."

Bridging the Divide

Over the next several weeks, Tony and I worked together to create a plan that would work for everyone. It wasn't easy. Finance and sales had always approached the business from different angles, but we found common ground in transparency.

Tony opened the books to the sales team, sharing detailed insights into our cost structure —labor, materials, and logistics. For many reps, it was the first time they truly understood what went into delivering the company's service. At the same time, I brought data from the field to Tony: competitive pressures, customer objections, and the challenges of holding the line on price.

In the end, we developed a blended compensation plan. Reps would still earn commissions on revenue, but they'd also receive bonuses for deals with margins above target thresholds. It wasn't perfect, but it aligned incentives without asking the reps to carry the weight of factors they couldn't control.

The transition wasn't smooth. Old habits die hard, and trust doesn't rebuild overnight. But as the months passed, the results started to show. Sales reps became more adept at defending prices. Margins stabilized, and Tony saw the numbers he needed.

I learned something crucial during that time. Leadership isn't about picking a side but finding the path that brings all sides together. Years later, when I became CEO, I often thought back to those meetings with Tony. The lessons we learned—about transparency, collaboration, and the power of perspective—helped shape how I led.

The story wasn't just about the company's margins or compensation plans. It was about trust and understanding—the building blocks of any successful team. And for me, it was a turning point in my journey from sales rep to CEO.

Building Bridges with Words

The Silent Killer: Misalignment

Sales reps see it every day. Marketing blames sales for not following up on leads. Operations grumble about overpromised delivery dates. Finance wants better forecasting. The result? Teams drift apart, productivity stalls, and everyone feels frustrated. Misalignment is a silent killer, but communication can bring teams' relationships back to life.

Speak to Their Needs

The best communicators adapt. Marketing wants to hear customer stories that validate campaigns. Finance listens when you speak in margins and revenue. Operations leans in when you clarify timelines. Tailor your message for each department, and they'll see you as a bridge instead of a barrier.

Start with Why

Simon Sinek popularized this idea, but it's timeless. People align when they know why something matters. When pitching an idea or updating your team, explain why it fits the company's vision. A sales rep who connects deals to the company's mission doesn't just close sales—they close gaps.

Show Up, Don't Just Speak Up

Technology makes it easy to send updates, but actual alignment comes from presence. Walk over to marketing. Have coffee with operations. Be in the room when decisions are made.

People align when they see you care enough to connect in person. If you work remote, use a video conferencing platform so that you can look people in the face.

Bridge the Divide

A true leader brings teams together. Host a meeting with marketing and sales to discuss shared goals. Use customer feedback to inform marketing campaigns. Break bread with operations to solve logistics challenges. Each small step builds a culture of trust and collaboration. But, as the next story shows, these principles came into sharp focus when I faced a high-stakes situation that tested my ability to align teams and deliver results.

Tuesdays Were the Product

Selling Time, Not Machines

When I started selling for Sightpath Medical, they first told me, "Our product isn't phaco machines; it's Tuesdays." That didn't make sense to me at first. I had spent years in sales, thinking in terms of quotas, equipment, and IOLs, not calendars. But the Sightpath model wasn't about hardware—it was about offering surgical days to surgeons who wanted the benefits of easy access to the newest technology without the burden of ownership.

The challenge was that there are only so many Tuesdays in a month—five, if we were lucky. Each of those Tuesdays represented surgical days that had to be coordinated between sales, operations, and the surgeons themselves. If I sold on a day we couldn't deliver, I'd burn credibility with the prospect, operations would resent me, and Sightpath would lose money.

My responsibility was to find a way to align our efforts—sales, operations, and the surgeon's expectations—so we could sell confidently and deliver consistently.

The Tuesday Tug-of-War

It all came to a head one summer. A promising prospect, a surgeon with three bustling clinics, was interested in bringing Sightpath into his rotation. He wanted three Tuesdays a month and wasn't shy about saying he'd walk if we couldn't guarantee them. I promised to make it happen.

But when I called operations to check availability, they laughed. "Joel," they said, "you can't just sell Tuesdays we don't have. The calendar is already tight. We're booked three months out, and your surgeon isn't even on the schedule yet."

I felt the familiar tug-of-war—sales pulling one way, operations pulling the other. If I pushed too hard, operations would balk, and I'd risk a strained relationship with them. If I didn't push enough, the surgeon would find someone else who could promise what he needed.

That night, I sat at my kitchen table, staring at a spreadsheet of available days, wondering how I could sell a vision that balanced ambition with reality. I had no room for error.

The Calendar Consensus

The answer came in the form of a plan that brought everyone to the table. The following day, I called the head of operations and suggested a joint meeting with their team and mine.

"Let's build a model together," I said, "so we're all looking at the same data."

During the meeting, I laid out the surgeon's needs and the potential revenue. I didn't sugarcoat the challenges. Operations countered with the reality of our capacity and the risks of overbooking. We went back and forth, but for the first time, it felt like collaboration, not competition.

Ultimately, we found a solution: offering the surgeon two Tuesdays and one Thursday. I called him to explain the plan, positioning the Thursday as a strategic move to accommodate his busiest clinic. He agreed, impressed by the transparency and the effort to meet his needs.

The deal closed. Operations delivered flawlessly, and the surgeon became one of our most loyal customers. But more than that, we had built a communication framework that outlasted the deal—a shared language of calendars and capacity that aligned our teams for the future.

The Importance of Alignment

In that moment, I learned that success wasn't just about selling the dream—it was about ensuring we could deliver it. By aligning sales and operations, I didn't just win a customer; I strengthened the business. It was a leadership lesson that stayed with me as I climbed toward the CEO chair: You can't grow a business without building bridges between teams. Sometimes, those bridges are made of Tuesdays.

Key Takeaway: The Power of a Clear Voice

Alignment isn't about control—it's about connection. When you communicate clearly and with purpose, you empower others to row in the same direction. Great leaders don't just talk; they bring people together with words that inspire trust, foster collaboration, and drive results.

Action Exercises

1. **Create a Department Alignment Plan:** Pick a project that requires input from multiple teams. Outline clear objectives, roles, and communication schedules for everyone involved. Review progress bi-weekly to ensure alignment and resolve conflicts.

2. **Practice Empathetic Communication:** Ask a colleague from another department what challenges they face. Listen actively, repeating back what you hear to confirm understanding. Suggest one way you can help or collaborate.

3. **Facilitate a Cross-Team Meeting:** Organize a meeting with sales, marketing, and operations. Discuss shared challenges and solutions. Close with agreed-upon actions that align with the company's goals.

23

What We Can Do Better: Lessons in Listening from Great CEOs

When you think of what makes a great CEO, fancy strategies and market domination might come to mind. But the truth is simpler and more profound. At its heart, the journey from sales rep to CEO hinges on mastering communication. Speak clearly. Be honest. Say what needs to be said, and people will follow.

The CEO Who Always Listened: How Sam Walton Built Walmart

Listening in the Aisles

In the early 1960s, Sam Walton, a driven entrepreneur and former sales rep for J.C. Penney, had a vision. He wanted to create a chain of stores where customers could find everything they needed at unbeatable prices. By 1962, his vision became a reality with the opening of the first Walmart in Rogers, Arkansas.

However, it wasn't just his business model that made Walmart different. Sam had a relentless belief that the best ideas didn't always come from the top. They came from the floor— where customers shopped, employees worked, and real problems unfolded. While other executives buried themselves in offices, Sam walked the aisles of his stores, stopping to ask his employees and customers a simple question: "What can we do better?"

The early days of Walmart were tough. Competitors were bigger, better funded, and already entrenched. Sam didn't have the resources to outspend them, but he had something else: his ability to listen. And he used it to learn everything he could about what people wanted and needed—whether they were customers, suppliers, or the employees running the cash registers.

The Day Sam Was Challenged

In 1979, Walmart was growing fast, but with growth came cracks in the foundation. One of Sam's regional managers approached him with bad news: Employee morale was slipping in key stores. Staff felt undervalued, unheard, and overwhelmed by the pressure to deliver results.

Customers, too, were starting to feel disconnected from the personalized service that had set Walmart apart in its early days.

Sam had always preached communication, but the message was getting lost as the business scaled. Employees no longer felt comfortable sharing their concerns, and managers weren't encouraging dialogue. Walmart risked becoming just another big-box retailer—a fate Sam had spent his career trying to avoid.

Sam decided to act immediately. He called a meeting of store managers from across the country and laid it out plainly: "We're only as good as our people. And if they don't feel heard, we're done. Starting today, we change that." His directive was clear: Every manager should spend more time listening to employees and customers.

The Saturday Morning Meetings

Sam didn't just talk about open communication—he institutionalized it. He launched "Saturday Morning Meetings," a tradition that became legendary at Walmart. Every Saturday, managers from all over the country gathered to share updates, exchange ideas, and troubleshoot issues. Employees and even store associates could have their voices heard in front of senior leadership. Sam himself often led these meetings, taking notes, asking questions, and making sure no voice was too small to be heard.

Sam also introduced his famous "10-Foot Rule," urging every employee to greet and assist anyone within 10 feet of them. It wasn't just about customer service but about creating a culture where every interaction mattered. Sam regularly visited stores unannounced, to talk to cashiers, stock clerks, and janitors, always asking the same question: "What's working, and what's not?"

The results were remarkable. By the mid-1980s, Walmart had become the largest retailer in the United States, and its culture of communication was a key driver. Employees felt valued, customers felt cared for, and the company stayed connected to the communities it served.

Sam's legacy wasn't just Walmart's success—he believed listening and communication were the ultimate competitive advantages. Even after his passing in 1992, his practices continued to define Walmart's culture.

Final Note

Sam Walton's story is a testament to the power of open communication. From his days as a sales rep to his rise as one of the most celebrated CEOs in history, Sam's success stemmed from his willingness to ask questions, listen to answers, and act on what he learned. His philosophy reminds us that whether you're leading a team of five or five thousand, communication isn't just a leadership skill—it's the foundation of success.

Why Communication Shapes Leadership

The greatest leaders know how to cut through the noise. They don't hide behind jargon or sugarcoat the truth. As a sales rep, if you aspire to be a CEO, you must learn this early: Communication isn't about talking more. It's about making your words count.

Clear communication builds bridges between departments, aligns strategies, and earns trust. Imagine you're in a meeting with marketing and operations. Each team is speaking their language—ROI metrics, operational constraints, sales targets. If you're the one who can listen, distill the chaos, and connect the dots, you become the person everyone looks to. That's leadership in action.

Transparency is equally vital. When things go wrong, the instinct might be to downplay the problem or shift the blame. Don't. Being upfront about challenges, whether with a customer or a colleague, doesn't just salvage relationships—it makes them stronger.

In my time leading teams, I've seen what happens when communication breaks down. A sales rep overpromises to a client. Operations scrambles to deliver. Marketing is left out of the loop and unable to help set expectations. The result? Frustration, finger-pointing, and lost trust. The fix was always the same: Clear, direct conversations to realign everyone. As a future CEO, you'll face moments like these on a grander scale. Practice now by being the voice of clarity and reason.

Good communication also isn't just about being heard—it's about hearing others. As Peter Drucker said, "The most important thing in communication is hearing what isn't said." Ask questions that matter. Listen to the answers. Dig deeper, and you'll uncover insights that others miss.

For sales reps, strong communication isn't just a skill; it's your ticket to the big leagues. The ability to communicate clearly and authentically—whether pitching a product, resolving a conflict, or rallying a team—makes you stand out. It positions you as more than a rep. It sets you on the path to leadership.

The CEO Who Spoke to Win: How Alan Mulally Saved Ford

A Company on the Brink

In 2006, Ford Motor Company was in freefall. The auto giant had lost billions, its stock price was cratering, and deep internal divides splintered the workforce. The situation looked bleak. Ford was losing its way, stuck in a web of fear, bureaucracy, and silos. Morale was low. Leaders avoided confronting the hard truths. It was into this storm that Alan Mulally, a calm yet determined man, walked in as the new CEO.

Mulally wasn't flashy. He didn't carry the mystique of a Silicon Valley innovator or the bravado of a Wall Street maverick. But what he brought was far more powerful: The courage to make communication the cornerstone of a corporate turnaround.

Breaking the Silence

Mulally's plan wasn't complex, but it challenged the very foundation of Ford's culture. He called it the "One Ford" vision—a simple, unifying strategy to align everyone from factory floor workers to C-suite executives. At its core was a weekly meeting where senior leaders would openly assess their progress using a color-coded system: green for success, yellow for caution, and red for problems.

At first, no one dared report a "red." Fear of failure ran deep. Executives danced around the truth, wary of showing weakness. Mulally knew this mindset was killing Ford. Change would only happen when leaders faced reality together.

Then, it happened. During one meeting, a brave executive admitted that his project was failing and marked it "red." The room froze. Expecting a lecture or reprimand, everyone turned to Mulally. What he did next changed everything.

He stood and clapped.

That single act shattered the wall of fear. Mulally wasn't punishing honesty—he was celebrating it. The red wasn't a mark of failure but a starting point for solutions. From then on, problems became opportunities, and transparency became the new normal.

Externally, Mulally simplified Ford's public message. He cut the clutter of corporate jargon, focusing instead on what Ford stood for: reliability, quality, and innovation. This clarity resonated, earning back customer trust. During the financial crisis of 2008, while competitors begged for bailouts, Ford's newfound transparency helped it secure loyalty from investors and customers alike.

A Culture Reborn

By the time Alan Mulally stepped down in 2014, Ford was a transformed company. It had returned to profitability, avoided bankruptcy, and rebuilt trust within and beyond its walls. Mulally's legacy wasn't built on revolutionary products or aggressive cost-cutting. Instead, it stemmed from his ability to foster a culture where honesty and communication drove results.

Mulally taught Ford's leaders—and the world—a powerful lesson: Communication isn't just about talking; it's about listening, aligning, and acting. And sometimes, the bravest thing a leader can do is clap for the truth.

This story of Alan Mulally showcases a simple truth for aspiring leaders: Clear, honest communication can be your most powerful tool. Whether you're leading a small sales territory or an iconic global brand, the ability to align your team through openness can turn chaos into clarity—and failure into success.

Key Takeaway: Speak Clearly, Listen Deeply

Communication and transparency are the building blocks of trust and credibility. Use them wisely, and they'll open doors to leadership. Speak clearly, listen deeply, and never shy away from honesty. These aren't just tools—they're habits that define great leaders. Build them now, and you'll be ready when your time comes.

Action Exercises

1. **Practice Active Listening:** During your next meeting, focus entirely on what others are saying without planning your response. Take notes and summarize their points back to them to ensure you've understood.

2. **Transparency Check-In:** Identify one area in your work where you've been hesitant to share information. Resolve to be upfront and see how it affects your relationships.

3. **Clear Message Challenge:** Write an email or memo summarizing a complex topic in five sentences or fewer. Share it with a colleague to see if they find it clear and actionable.

24

The Humble Road to High Office: How Seeking Humility Leads to the Top

You may think the key to success lies in confidence, charm, or relentless drive. But what if the real key is something quieter, something often overlooked? Seeking humility—actively striving to understand your place in the bigger picture—might be the most powerful tool for transforming your career and life.

Lessons from the Prodigal Son: A Framework for Leadership and Life

The Call to Lunch

It was a cold day in early 2011 when I drove to the Franciscan friary in Prior Lake, Minnesota, to meet my friend, Father Howard Hansen. A Franciscan priest nearing the end of his life, Father Howard had a way of making every interaction feel profound. I was in my mid-forties, busy climbing my career ladder, and our lunches were a welcome pause from the hustle.

When I arrived, the friary director met me in the modest lobby. His expression was somber as he explained that Father Howard was too ill to leave his room. "He'd still like to see you," the director added. "He wants to have lunch with you in his room."

I hesitated, not knowing what to expect. Franciscan friars' rooms are known for their simplicity: a bed, a desk, a chair. I wondered where we would eat and if the experience might be too much for Father Howard in his current condition. The director assured me they had everything taken care of, and Father Howard was looking forward to my visit.

The Painting on the Wall

Father Howard's room was as sparse as I'd imagined—small, with only the essentials. Yet my eyes were immediately drawn to a framed print on the wall. It was a copy of Rembrandt's *The Return of the Prodigal Son*. The warmth of its brushstrokes stood in complete contrast to the starkness of the room.

As we began our lunch, I couldn't hold back my curiosity. "Tell me about that painting," I asked.

He smiled, his face lighting up despite his frailty. "Ah, Joel," he began, "this painting has been one of my life's greatest teachers." His voice was soft but deliberate.

Over the next two hours, Father Howard poured out his heart. He spoke of the characters in the painting—the father's mercy, the prodigal son's shame and hope, the elder brother's resentment—and how he had seen himself in each of them at different times in his life.

Tears welled in his eyes as he recounted moments of humility, failure, and forgiveness.

Then he laughed, remembering times when stubbornness had held him back, only for grace to pull him forward. Each story was like a thread, weaving the fabric of a life lived with reflection and meaning.

I listened, humbled by his vulnerability. Father Howard wasn't lecturing; he shared the raw truth of being human.

A Framework for Life

Two months later, Father Howard passed away. The framed *Prodigal Son* stayed etched in my mind. Its lessons lingered, urging me to reflect on my own decisions, relationships, and leadership.

Around that time, I began reading Peter Drucker's works. Drucker's focus on management, innovation, and leadership complemented Father Howard's spiritual wisdom in ways I couldn't have predicted. One offered practical frameworks; the other, a moral compass.

Together, they began to form an operating system for my life and career.

Today, I keep small reproductions of *The Return of the Prodigal Son* near my desks at work and home. Each time I face a difficult decision, I look at that painting. Am I the father, offering grace? Am I the prodigal son, seeking redemption? Or am I the elder brother, stuck in pride? The answer often surprises me.

Father Howard's stories and Drucker's philosophies may seem worlds apart. Still, together, they remind me of what leadership truly means: To lead is to serve, to forgive, and to seek clarity, even in the most chaotic moments. That lesson has guided me from sales rep to CEO, and I strive to carry it out every day.

The next time you encounter a challenge—at work or in life—consider who you are in the story of the prodigal son. Are you showing mercy? Seeking it? Or resisting it? The answers may shape not just your decisions but the leader you are becoming.

Humility as an Operating System for Success

The Quiet Power of Humility

True humility isn't about diminishing yourself. It's about clear-eyed honesty— recognizing your strengths, acknowledging your weaknesses, and staying open to growth. It means thinking less about your own image and more about the value you bring to others.

Humility forces you to ask, "What don't I know?" That question doesn't weaken you; it makes you stronger. It creates room for learning and positions you as someone who values truth over ego. Customers trust you more. Colleagues see you as approachable. Leaders notice your focus on solutions rather than self-promotion.

The Business Case for Humility

Sales reps who embody humility naturally build trust. They listen more than they talk, seek feedback, and use it to improve. They admit when they're wrong, which earns respect and clears the path to better solutions. This mindset, adopted early, shapes the trajectory toward becoming a respected leader.

Father Cajetan Mary de Bergamo's *Humility of Heart* teaches that humility is the root of all virtue. In business, this means cultivating a culture where egos take a backseat to collaboration. When teams prioritize ideas over ownership, creativity flourishes. When leaders model humility, they empower others to shine.

Leading with Humble Confidence

Humility and confidence aren't opposites—they're allies. Confidence rooted in humility isn't arrogant—it's steady. It says, "I trust my abilities, but I'm willing to learn from anyone." This kind of leadership inspires loyalty and courage in others. It turns mistakes into lessons and victories into collective achievements.

Humility is an indispensable tool for a sales rep aiming for the CEO seat. It's not about waiting your turn to lead; it's about earning the trust that makes others want to follow you.

A Leader's Quiet Strength

The Gentle Teacher

When I first met Scott Hussey at Upsher-Smith Laboratories, I didn't yet understand what made a truly great sales manager—or a great leader, for that matter. But Scott had a calm presence that set him apart. He wasn't flashy or overbearing. Instead, he was patient. Humble. He was the kind of person who made you want to work harder, not because he demanded it, but because you respected him.

As a team of young, eager sales reps, we were raw and inexperienced. Scott didn't seem fazed by that. He took the time to teach us how to sell—not by spouting scripts or playing clever games with doctors but by listening, learning, and offering something of value.

At the time, I thought Scott's calm demeanor was just his nature. I didn't know there was more behind it.

Strength Forged in Loss

Partway through my year at Upsher-Smith, everything changed. Scott's wife became gravely ill. He didn't share much about it with the team—he wasn't the kind of man to make his burdens public. But we could see it in his eyes and the way his shoulders carried an invisible weight.

Even then, Scott stayed the same for us. He showed up. He coached us. He focused on what we needed, even as his world fell apart. Watching him endure that time with quiet grace was the first time I really saw what humility and strength looked like. It wasn't loud or dramatic. It didn't seek recognition.

Scott had a young son to care for and a wife he was losing. Yet he still found ways to serve. A devout Catholic, Scott leaned on his faith and something bigger than himself. He didn't let his personal struggles stop him from being a leader—not just to us but to everyone who relied on him.

When his wife passed away shortly after I left the company, I wasn't there to see how he carried on. But I knew he would, the way only someone with unshakable inner strength could.

Legacy of Leadership

Years later, our paths crossed again. By then, I had moved on in my career, but Scott remained the same in essence. We were both members of St. Hubert's Catholic Church in Chanhassen, Minnesota.

Scott had remarried and started a new chapter of his life, now raising two more children alongside his first son. As before, he was a leader—not just in business, but in the community.

He generously gave his time and resources, becoming a pillar of strength for others.

Seeing Scott again reminded me of what I learned from him during those early days. Leadership isn't about shouting the loudest or demanding the most. It's about showing up—day after day, even when it's hard. It's about serving others, staying humble, and drawing strength from something greater than yourself.

Scott's quiet example continues to inspire me. In many ways, he taught me not just how to sell but also how to lead—and, ultimately, how to live.

Key Takeaway: The Unfinished Work of Seeking Humility

Seeking humility isn't a goal to check off a list. It's a way of being. Every challenge you face as a sales rep or a leader offers a chance to learn, adapt, and grow. The pursuit keeps you honest, keeps you learning, and keeps you human. Humility isn't the absence of strength—it's the foundation of wisdom. You build a foundation for trust, growth, and authentic leadership by embracing humility as your operating system. Remember, seeking humility isn't about being perfect—it's about striving for better every day; the same striving that will lead you from sales rep to CEO.

Action Exercises

1. **Daily Humility Check-In:** Each night, write down one instance where you felt pride taking the lead. Reflect on how a more humble approach might have changed the interaction. Decide one step to take tomorrow to align more closely with humility.

2. **Customer Conversations with Curiosity:** During your next three sales calls, focus on asking open-ended questions. Resist the urge to dominate the conversation. Reflect on what you learned by genuinely listening.

3. **Public Recognition Exercise:** At your next team meeting, publicly thank a colleague for their contributions. Be specific about what they did and how it mattered. Reflect on how this shifts your perspective as a leader.

Conclusion

The journey of this book is over, but your own path from sales rep to CEO is only just beginning. I sincerely hope that within the book you've found some direction, inspiration, and actionable strategies that will help you discover that transformation and unlock your potential to be a leader who changes lives.

In Part One, we saw the importance of vision, strategy, and goals for companies and CEOs. I hope those chapters have helped to clarify your vision and goals for your own career and given you strategies that you can use to achieve them.

In Part Two, we saw how crucial understanding yourself is as a beginning step in your journey to the corner office. I hope that section showed you how cultivating a growth mindset and adopting an ethos of service are essential steps toward success.

In Part Three, we examined the importance of understanding the organization as a whole, showing how that knowledge positions you to lead it. I hope that part deepened your belief in the power of the role played by organizational culture, systems, and processes, and illustrated how you can influence each of those elements as part of your own transformation into a leadership role.

In Part Four, we explored the importance of learning about core functions including finance and marketing. I hope those chapters inspired you to learn more about the other disciplines that you must understand if you are to fulfill your potential as both a sales rep and a CEO.

In Part Five, we moved beyond the organization to focus on the world in which it operates. I hope my discussions of metrics and understanding customers pointed helpfully toward ways in which you can develop your career and rise to the top of the organization.

Lastly, in Part Six, we returned to you, with a survey of the attributes of a leader, highlighting the importance of transparency, honest communication, and, most crucially of all, humility. Paradoxically, in my experience, the humble road is the best way to the greatest achievements.

Following this conclusion, the resources section lists further sources that you can turn to for additional inspiration and guidance on your journey of personal and career development. I have also included a 100-day action plan, setting out what you can do immediately to start your journey to the top.

Finally, I'd like to return to the question with which this book began and to encourage you to ask yourself once again, "Why not me?" I sincerely hope that everything you have read since then has shown you that you can transform yourself from sales rep to CEO. But ultimately, my experiences and those of the many mentors who have inspired me can only point you in the right direction. It's up to you to walk the path in your own unique way. With new ideas in your head and new belief in your heart, I encourage you to take the first step today.

How to Get Your Free Guide: "The 3 CEO Skills Every Sales Rep Needs"

If you're serious about taking your sales career to the next level, I've created a free companion guide to this book just for you.

In The 3 CEO Skills Every Sales Rep Needs, you'll discover:

1. How to think like a CEO and make smarter business decisions

2. How to sell to executives and close bigger deals

3. How to lead without a title and position yourself for leadership

Download your free copy now at:

https://www.joelgaslin.com/the-three-ceo-skills-every-sales-rep-needs/

This guide will help you put these skills into action immediately—so you can start making the mindset shift from *sales rep* to *future CEO*. And after that, we can talk about getting you into The Sales Rep to CEO Masterclass!

Further Reading

Part One—Understanding Vision, Strategy, and Goals

1. *Start with Why* by Simon Sinek
2. *The Advantage* by Patrick Lencioni
3. *Built to Last* by Jim Collins and Jerry I. Porras
4. *The Vision-Driven Leader* by Michael Hyatt
5. *Good Strategy/Bad Strategy* by Richard Rumelt
6. *Playing to Win* by A.G. Lafley and Roger L. Martin
7. *Blue Ocean Strategy* by W. Chan Kim and Renée Mauborgne
8. *The Art of Strategy* by Avinash K. Dixit and Barry J. Nalebuff
9. *Visionary Business* by Marc Allen
10. *Measure What Matters* by John Doerr

Part Two—Understanding Yourself

1. *Mindset* by Carol Dweck

2. *Grit* by Angela Duckworth

3. *Peak* by Anders Ericsson and Robert Pool

4. *Atomic Habits* by James Clear

5. *The Obstacle Is the Way* by Ryan Holiday

6. *The Go-Giver* by Bob Burg and John David Mann

7. *Leaders Eat Last* by Simon Sinek

8. *Give and Take* by Adam Grant

9. *Raving Fans* by Ken Blanchard and Sheldon Bowles

10. *Good to Great* by Jim Collins

11. *The Effective Executive* by Peter Drucker

12. *The Five Dysfunctions of a Team* by Patrick Lencioni

Part Three—Understanding Your Organization

1. *Drive* by Daniel H. Pink

2. *The Culture Code* by Daniel Coyle

3. *Tribal Leadership* by Dave Logan, John King, and Halee Fischer-Wright

4. *The Long and the Short of It* by Peter Field and Les Binet

5. *The Challenger Sale* by Matthew Dixon and Brent Adamson

6. *Customer Success* by Nick Mehta, Dan Steinman, and Lincoln Murphy

7. *The Trusted Advisor* by David H. Maister, Charles H. Green, and Robert M. Galford

8. *Building a StoryBrand* by Donald Miller

9. *The E-Myth Revisited* by Michael E. Gerber

10. *Getting Things Done* by David Allen

11. *Deep Work* by Cal Newport

Part Four—Understanding Finance, Pricing, and Marketing

1. *Financial Intelligence for Entrepreneurs* by Karen Berman and Joe Knight

2. *The Personal MBA* by Josh Kaufman

3. *The Essential Drucker* by Peter Drucker

4. *The New One Minute Manager* by Ken Blanchard and Spencer Johnson

5. *Understanding Business Accounting for Dummies* by Colin Barrow

6. *What the CEO Wants You to Know* by Ram Charan

7. *Profit First* by Mike Michalowicz

8. *Negotiation Genius* by Deepak Malhotra and Max H. Bazerman.

9. *Predictable Revenue* by Aaron Ross and Marylou Tyler

10. *They Ask You Answer* by Marcus Sheridan

11. *This Is Marketing* by Seth Godin

12. *Aligned to Achieve* by Tracy Eiler and Andrea Austin

13. *Killing Marketing* by Joe Pulizzi and Robert Rose

14. *Hacking Sales* by Max Altschuler

Part Five—Understanding the World Around You

1. *SPIN Selling* by Neil Rackham

2. *Cracking the Sales Management Code* by Jason Jordan and Michelle Vazzana

3. *Buyer Personas* by Adele Revella

4. *To Sell Is Human* by Daniel Pink

5. *Content Inc.* by Joe Pulizzi

6. *Made to Stick* by Chip Heath and Dan Heath

Part Six—Understanding the Attributes of a Leader

1. *Cardiac Arrest* by Howard Root

2. *The Speed of Trust* by Stephen M.R. Covey

3. *Radical Candor* by Kim Scott

4. *Integrity* by Henry Cloud

5. *Trust and Betrayal in the Workplace* by Dennis S. Reina and Michelle L. Reina

6. *Crucial Conversations* by Kerry Patterson, Joseph Grenny, Ron McMillan, and Al Switzler

7. *Trust Works!* by Ken Blanchard

8. *Integrity Selling for the 21st Century* by Ron Willingham

9. *Extreme Ownership* by Jocko Willink and Leif Babin

10. *Leadership and Self-Deception* by The Arbinger Institute

11. *"What Makes a Leader?"* by Daniel Goleman (Harvard Business Review article)

12. *Dare to Lead* by Brené Brown

13. *The Ideal Team Player* by Patrick Lencioni

14. *Humilitas* by John Dickson

15. *Ego is the Enemy* by Ryan Holiday

16. *Humility of Heart* by Father Cajetan Mary de Bergamo

100-Day Plan: Your Path to Becoming a Sales Rep CEO

Phase 1: Foundation & Awareness (Days 1-25)

Objective: Build a strong foundation of mindset, vision, and customer understanding.

Actions:

1. Define Your Vision and Strategy

- Draft a vision statement for your sales territory.
- Identify key opportunities and potential threats.
- Align this vision with company objectives.

2. Establish Key Metrics

- Track revenue growth, new customer acquisition, and conversion rates.
- Begin monitoring customer churn rate—identify how many customers leave, why they leave, and the revenue impact.

3. Make Friends in Finance & Marketing

- Set up meetings with finance and marketing teams.
- Learn how customer churn impacts company revenue and profitability.
- Work with marketing to identify messaging strategies that improve customer retention.

4. Cultivate a Service Mindset

- Shift from transactional selling to a service-driven approach.
- Assess your customer interactions—are you focused on their long-term success or just making the sale?

5. Analyze Your Existing Customer Base

- Review customer history and identify those at risk of churn.
- Understand what differentiates your most loyal customers from those who leave.

Phase 2: Execution & Market Impact (Days 26-60)

Objective: Deepen customer relationships, refine strategies, and test new approaches.

Actions:

6. Deep Dive into Churn Drivers

- Conduct exit interviews or surveys with lost customers.
- Categorize churn reasons (pricing, poor experience, unmet expectations, competitor influence).
- Identify internal processes that may contribute to churn.

7. Develop Retention Strategies

- Offer added value rather than price discounts to retain customers.
- Implement personalized check-ins with at-risk customers.
- Collaborate with marketing to create targeted content addressing common concerns.

8. Expand High-Value Customer Engagement

- Identify and nurture your most valuable customers.
- Strengthen partnerships with long-term clients through additional training, support, or exclusive offers.
- Leverage successful customers as advocates to reduce churn risk.

9. Enhance Transparency in Financial Discussions

- Improve how you communicate pricing, value, and ROI with customers.
- Discuss potential pricing changes or contract adjustments proactively to avoid churn surprises.

10. Seek Humility in Learning & Innovation

- Adapt sales approaches based on customer feedback.
- Stay open to new ways of engaging and supporting customers.

Phase 3: Mastery & Leadership (Days 61-100)

Objective: Reinforce long-term strategies, establish leadership influence, and drive sustainable growth.

Actions:

11. Create an Ongoing Churn Prevention System

- Work with customer success teams to proactively monitor customer satisfaction.
- Set up automated check-ins for key customers.
- Track churn reduction progress and adjust strategies as needed.

12. Refine Your Personal Sales & Leadership Brand

- Position yourself as a trusted advisor, not just a sales rep.
- Share industry insights and best practices with customers.
- Become the go-to resource for problem-solving in your industry.

13. Train Others in What You've Learned

- Share successful churn-reduction strategies with colleagues.
- Host a lunch-and-learn session on retention techniques.

14. Evaluate Your Progress

- Compare results against initial benchmarks from Phase 1.
- Identify lessons learned and areas for continued improvement.

15. Set the Next 100-Day Growth Plan

- Expand focus beyond churn to new opportunities for increasing customer lifetime value.
- Identify leadership opportunities to implement what you've learned at a larger scale.